Progress to Proficiency
Teacher's Book

Progress
to Proficiency

Teacher's Book

Leo Jones

CAMBRIDGE
UNIVERSITY PRESS

Published by the Press Syndicate of the University of Cambridge
The Pitt Building, Trumpington Street, Cambridge CB2 1RP
40 West 20th Street, New York, NY 10011–4211, USA
10 Stamford Road, Oakleigh, Victoria 3166, Australia

© Cambridge University Press 1986

First published 1986
Eighth printing 1992

Printed in Great Britain
at the University Press, Cambridge

ISBN 0 521 31343 0 Teacher's Book
ISBN 0 521 31342 2 Student's Book
ISBN 0 521 30850 X Set of 2 cassettes

Contents

Thanks

My special thanks to Christine Cairns and Alison Silver for all their hard work, friendly encouragement and editorial expertise.

Thanks also to all the teachers and students at the following schools and institutes who used the pilot edition of this book and made so many helpful comments and suggestions: The Bell School in Cambridge, the British Council Institute in Barcelona, The British School in Florence, the College of Arts and Technology in Newcastle upon Tyne, the Eurocentre in Cambridge, Godmer House in Oxford, the Hampstead Garden Suburb Institute in London, Inlingua Brighton & Hove, International House in Arezzo, Klubschule Migros in St Gallen, The Moraitis School in Athens, the Moustakis School of English in Athens, the Newnham Language Centre in Cambridge, VHS Aachen, VHS Heidelberg, VHS Karlsruhe, the Wimbledon School of English in London and Ray Thomson in Switzerland. Without their help and reassurance this book could not have taken shape.

The author and publishers are grateful to the following who have given permission for the use of copyright material identified in the text: 4.2 Collins Publishers and A. D. Peters & Co. for the extract from *The Towers of Trebizond* by Rose Macaulay; 9.6 *The Guardian*; 16.6 David Simpson and *The Guardian*.

Introduction

Progress to Proficiency is for any group of students preparing for the University of Cambridge Certificate of Proficiency in English examination. It contains a wide variety of practice activities and exercises which increase in difficulty and complexity unit by unit until, towards the end, students are tackling tasks of exam standard.

The aim of the book is to help students to learn the language skills they need to do well in the Proficiency exam – to learn by 'doing' (ie by actively using their English) and not by passively expecting to 'be taught'. Varied and interesting practice increases students' confidence and flexibility and also allows them to discover what they still need to learn to improve.

At Proficiency level a traditional course book (with its long, detailed explanations of grammar points, advice on how to write a good essay, descriptions of appropriate style and so on) is unwieldly and time-consuming. The best source of such explanations and advice is not a book but the teacher. The teacher is the person who knows the class personally: only the teacher knows what their strengths and weaknesses are, what they know already and what their interests and enthusiasms are. Only the teacher knows what kind of action to take when difficulties arise – perhaps action as straightforward as suggesting better ways of saying or writing things, or more complex such as introducing suitable supplementary material. No textbook writer can replace the teacher because the problems any particular group of students will have are individual and unpredictable. The teacher therefore has a creative contribution to make – not just by regulating the pace and intensity of each lesson, but by adapting the material to the class's needs and interests, by giving the right kind of advice and by maintaining a good working atmosphere.

Students at this level cannot expect to be 'taught', they have to 'learn' – that is by asking questions, by discovering for themselves, by reading widely, by drawing on each other's knowledge, by finding out what they can do well and what they are weak at, but above all by discovering how to use the English they already know in a flexible way to perform a wide range of tasks.

Examination practice tests (or old exam papers), though helpful to accustom students to what they should expect in the exam, are not suitable for classroom use for a number of reasons:
– the questions are based on a random selection of different language points, which is confusing for students;

1

- many of the questions seem impossibly hard (only the best candidates will get them right) while others seem ridiculously easy (to give marks to the weakest candidates), and this is frustrating for students;
- the texts are chosen because they are suitable for testing purposes, not because they are intrinsically interesting;
- no help whatsoever is given to help students to improve their performance.

By contrast, *Progress to Proficiency* provides comprehensive and, above all, systematic coverage of the wide range of language skills required in the Proficiency exam. Some of the exercises are simply designed to help students to learn, some provide a challenge so that they will 'stretch' their English, some provide opportunities for discussion. The texts have been chosen because they are likely to interest, entertain, inform, provoke or intrigue students. The course is designed to help students to progressively improve their skills in the different areas tested in the exam.

In a Proficiency course there has to be a realistic balance between exam preparation (after all, everyone wants to do well in the exam!) and improving language skills that will be useful in the real world. The material in this book will make sure that this balance is maintained throughout the course. This is why each exercise in the book frankly and unashamedly declares its relationship to a particular part of the exam (eg 5.4 Linking words: *Use of English*). Students are thus aware of the aim of each exercise and can measure the progress they are making from unit to unit. This will not be felt as a restriction since the exercises and activities are themselves enjoyable and several different language skills are required to complete each one.

Most of the exercises can be done in class with students working together in pairs or small groups. Working together in this way has several important advantages:
- it enables students to discuss their answers to the questions and exchange opinions, thus developing an inquisitive and critical attitude without expecting every question to have one obviously perfect correct answer;
- students are more active and stay more alert than they would if the exercises were done 'round the class', with most students sitting and waiting for their turn to come round;
- it's easier to remember things you have found out for yourself than things you've been told or read about;
- students learn from each other.

The 18 topics in *Progress to Proficiency* have been selected not just because they 'come up' in the Proficiency exam but because they are important for advanced learners. No apologies are made for including such topics as 'Politics', 'Business and work' or 'Science and technology' because these are areas which any educated English speaker should be confident enough to read about, hear about and discuss – not as an expert or as a professional, but as an informed lay person.

Teachers familiar with *Progress towards First Certificate* will notice that this book retains many of its more effective and enjoyable features. However, thanks to the higher level of the Proficiency exam and the wider number of topics required, students are set free to explore areas that are more intellectually demanding and probably more stimulating. In both books the exercises are arranged in a similar way, but here the Composition exercises are left to the end of the unit, by which time students will have consolidated their ideas and opinions on the topic concerned. The larger number of units has enabled me to alternate some Use of English and Interview exercises in odd- and even-numbered units (see below).

As you work through the book, you will become aware of a 'progression' or development from unit to unit:
— from   exercises where the questions can be discussed
   to   exam-style questions;
— from   exercises with problems to be solved with a partner
   to   exercises which have to be done alone;
— from   exercises where guidance is given
   to   exercises where students have to use their own acquired knowledge;
— from   exercises which help students to learn
   to   exercises which, like the exam, test their knowledge;
— from   exercises where students work at their own speed
   to   exercises which have to be done within exam-style constraints of time and length.
Hence the title: **Progress** *to Proficiency.*

To do all the exercises in one unit takes about 5 or 6 hours – longer if a lot of time is devoted to discussion. The whole course thus requires 90 to 110 hours to complete, though students who are willing to spend time preparing exercises at home may not need so long. Any substantial pieces of written work (ie compositions and summaries) will, it is assumed, be done as homework in any case.

How the exercises work

1 Vocabulary

Each unit begins with an exercise on vocabulary, designed to help students to expand their command of English lexis and to show how different lexical items are used. Inevitably an exercise of this type is to some extent a test, if only because no two students share the same knowledge of English. However, different students will benefit from different parts of each exercise: learning new words, being reminded of words they don't actively use, finding words with similar meanings and determining how they are used.

There is a progression in the book

from exercises which introduce and practise vocabulary without reference to the exam

to exercises with sentences where the end of each word is m.issing............. or even the whole word is ...missing.....

to exercises where students have to choose three synonymous words from a choice of

five √ 5√ three two 3 + 2 √

to exercises with exam-style multiple-choice questions where only .... alternative is correct.

one√ · two three four

to exercises where there are also questions on grammar and usage, as in the exam.

These vocabulary exercises alone are *not* sufficient to expand students' vocabulary adequately: they also need to be encouraged to read widely – fiction and non-fiction, books, newspapers and magazines in English. They should also possess a good dictionary, such as the *Longman Dictionary of Contemporary English* or the *Oxford Advanced Learner's Dictionary of Current English*, and be able to use it efficiently.

The Teacher's Book contains answer keys and suggestions for handling these exercises, together with discussion ideas.

2 and 3   Reading

Each unit contains two reading comprehension exercises. The passages have been chosen because they are interesting, well-written and a pleasure to read. Some are easy to read, others more difficult. They are all taken from authentic sources (books, newspapers, magazines, etc.) and are reproduced exactly as they originally appeared or slightly rearranged to fit the page format of this book. Most of the texts from works of fiction are the opening paragraphs of a book – this is intended to whet the reader's appetite and encourage further reading.

The questions focus on different aspects of the reading skill: reading for gist or reading to extract specific information, as well as recognising and appreciating the style of the passage and the writer's attitude or intention.

There is a progression unit by unit

from exercises where students are asked questions like this:

Who made the first move? Harry

or The person who made the first move was ...Harry............

or true/false questions:

Harry was the one who made the first move. T

to multiple-choice questions:

The one who made the first move was ....
Harry √   Henry   Holly   Hetty

Each reading comprehension exercise has more questions than would be asked in an exam, where candidates' understanding is 'sampled' only. To save time in class, students may be asked to prepare the reading passages by reading them through at home beforehand.

The Teacher's Book contains background information on the writers whose work is reproduced, an answer key and suggestions for class discussion.

4 and 5   Use of English

In even-numbered units there is a grammatical transformation exercise and a gap-filling grammar exercise; in odd-numbered units there is a cloze exercise, based on an authentic text, and an exercise on phrasal verbs and idioms. Doing these exercises enables students to assess their knowledge of all the main areas of English grammar and usage that are tested in Paper 3 of the Proficiency examination. If they find that they are particularly weak in certain areas, or are puzzled by them, they should refer to *Practical English Usage* by Michael Swan (OUP) or a similar reference grammar. There are no long, discursive grammatical explanations in these exercises since these would take up a great deal of space and can be found elsewhere (just as explanations of vocabulary would be found in a dictionary).

There is a progression in these exercises
from   exercises where students are given clues (such as a list of suitable prepositions to use to fill the gaps)
to   exercises where no clues are given, but which still focus on one particular area of grammar.

The themes of each exercise are as follows:

Transformation exercises	Gap-filling exercises
2.4 Reporting speech	2.5 Verbs followed by -ing, to . . . or that . . .
4.4 Positive and negative sentences	4.5 Comparative and superlative sentences
6.4 Past, present and future forms	6.5 Reporting speech
8.4 Conditional sentences	8.5 Linking words and phrases
10.4 Obligation, necessity and probability	10.5 Word order and inversion
12.4 Reported speech	12.5 Linking words and phrases
14.4 Requests and politeness	14.5 Uses of the past tense
16.4 The passive and question tags	16.5 Aspects of the future
18.3 Exam-style transformations	18.4 Exam-style gap-filling

Cloze gap-filling exercises	Phrasal verb and idiom exercises
1.4 Prepositions	1.5 Idioms with TAKE
3.4 Articles	3.5 Idioms with GET
5.4 Linking words	5.5 Idioms with PUT
7.4 Prepositions and particles	7.5 Idioms with GO
9.4 Collocations	9.5 Idioms with COME
11.4 Prepositions and particles	11.5 Idioms with KEEP and GIVE
13.4 Collocations	13.5 Idioms with BREAK, BRING and CALL
15.4 Exam-style cloze exercise	15.5 Idioms with MAKE
17.4 Exam-style cloze exercise	17.5 Idioms with RUN and STAND

Any of these exercises can be done by students working together in class or set as homework and discussed later in class.

The Teacher's Book contains an answer key to the exercises.

6 Questions and summary

Every unit has an exercise where the comprehension questions on a passage have to be answered in complete written sentences and a summary has to be written, in preparation for Section B of the Use of English paper. The texts used are all taken from authentic sources. The questions focus attention on explaining the meaning of certain words used in the passage, explaining the reference of cataphoric and anaphoric devices (such as 'it' or 'this'), as well as selecting relevant information and writing a summary. Normally these exercises would be done orally by students working together before the answers are written down, probably as homework.

There is a progression unit by unit
from exercises where only a few questions have to be answered and a very short summary is required
to exercises requiring a summary of a certain length (eg 50 words)
to exam-style exercises with a variety of questions requiring written answers

The Teacher's Book contains an answer key in the form of notes and some ideas for class discussion, together with background information where necessary.

7 and 8   Listening

Each unit contains two listening exercises. A wide variety of simulated authentic texts are used: broadcasts, conversations, interviews, discussions and monologues. The questions focus attention on listening for gist as well as listening for specific information and determining the attitude of the speakers.

Students will normally need to hear each recording at least twice – some of the exercises have two parts with different tasks to be completed as they listen to the recording for the first and then for the second time. These exercises will be more 'sociable' if students compare notes with a partner after they have heard the recording each time.

As the exam may include a variety of question types, these listening exercises include: exercises with true/false questions, exercises with open-ended questions, exercises where the answers have to be shown graphically, exercises where a form or chart has to be completed and exercises with multiple-choice questions.

There is a progression unit by unit
from exercises that are relatively easy to understand, with straightforward questions on the content
to exercises that are more difficult to understand, with more demanding questions that may catch out the unwary student

The Teacher's Book contains a complete transcript of the recordings and an answer key, together with ideas for class discussion.
(One of the listening exercises can be done at the beginning of each unit, as suggested in the Teacher's Book. This may provide variety and seem less 'formidable' than starting with the Vocabulary exercise every time.)

9   Picture conversation / Pronunciation

A Picture Conversation exercise in odd-numbered units alternates with a Pronunciation exercise in even-numbered units. These exercises are at the back of the Student's Book in scrambled form among the 'communication activities', so that there is an information gap between the partners. In the Picture Conversations, one partner finds out about the other's photo by asking questions. In the Pronunciation exercises, each partner has a different extract from an authentic text to read aloud and later discuss. Reading aloud is an extremely effective way of helping students to improve their pronunciation (which will be assessed in the exam) and students at this level must be able to read clearly and comprehensibly.

During these exercises, go from group to group offering advice on vocabulary and pronunciation. Draw attention to grammatical or phonological errors. They should also discuss the *content* of the texts. Later, perhaps get one group to 'perform' in front of the rest of the class.

There is a progression from unit to unit in the amount of guidance given and in the difficulty of the tasks. The Teacher's Book contains a brief description of each exercise.

Picture Conversations in the communication activities section:

1.9: 1 + 37	11.9: 19 + 54
3.9: 3 + 42	13.9: 23 + 49
5.9: 26 + 44	15.9: 28 + 66
7.9: 13 + 51	17.9: 35 + 70
9.9: 16 + 59	18.7: 36 + 72

Pronunciation exercises in the communication activities section:

2.9: 2 + 40	12.9: 21 + 61
4.9: 4 + 45 + 71	14.9: 27 + 65 + 78
6.9: 10 + 48 + 77	16.9: 32 + 43
8.9: 15 + 53 + 74	18.7: 24 + 41
10.9: 18 + 57	

10 Communication activity

In every unit there is a communication activity, where students use the language and ideas they have encountered in the unit in a discussion, information gap activity or problem-solving activity. These activities are 'scrambled' at the back of the Student's Book, so that the partners (working in pairs or groups of three) cannot see each other's information.

There is a progression from unit to unit in the amount of information given and the amount of imaginative input required from the students. The Teacher's Book contains a brief description of each activity.

Communication activities:

1.10: 7 + 39	7.10: 14 + 52	13.10: 25 + 63
2.10: 5 + 38	8.10: 12 or 55	14.10: 29 + 64 + 75
3.10: 6 + 73 + 79	9.10: 17 + 56	15.10: 30 + 67
4.10: 8 + 47 + 76	10.10: (in main text)	16.10: 33 + 68
5.10: 9 + 46	11.10: 20 + 60	17.10: 34 + 69
6.10: 11 + 50 (also answer key to 6.6 in 58 and 31)	12.10: 22 + 62	18.7: (in main text)

11 Composition

These exercises cover all the types of composition and essay required in the Proficiency exam: descriptive, narrative, discursive – as well as shorter more specific tasks where students are expected to write a report or a letter. The ideas students may wish to express in their compositions will have been developed and discussed in earlier exercises in the unit, particularly in the

8

Interview exercises, so by the time they reach this exercise they will be ready to express these ideas in writing. The exercises are designed to be discussed beforehand and afterwards. It is recommended that completed compositions are not just handed in for the teacher to evaluate but also given to other members of the class to read.

There is a progression from unit to unit
from   exercises where students write at a length they feel comfortable
to   exercises where students are given guidance and information on which to base their writing
to   exercises where students write compositions of exam length (200 or 350 words) and against the clock

The Teacher's Book contains, for each unit, some advice on a different aspect of 'good writing' which students should have their attention drawn to, covering the following points:
a good introduction, using paragraphs, register, selection and ordering of information, making notes, correct spelling, punctuation, precise and appropriate vocabulary, a good conclusion, linking words, short and long sentences, interesting adjectives, attitude words, relevance to the question asked, overall structure, and grammatical accuracy.

Students who have particular difficulties with composition writing should refer to *Writing Skills* by Norman Coe, Robin Rycroft and Pauline Ernest (CUP) or *Writing Tasks* by David Jolly (CUP) for extra practice.

In marking students' compositions, don't just underline all the errors – show each student what they did well and what they need to improve to bring their work to Proficiency standard. Remember that it's the effect of a complete composition that is important, not all its little defects, and covering a student's work in masses of red ink is likely to be more discouraging than helpful.

Prescribed reading

Progress to Proficiency does not contain questions on particular books, as these change each year. However in unit 8 students are given an opportunity both to discuss one of the prescribed books and write about it. Choosing one of these books not only gives students an extra topic to choose from in Paper 2 and to talk about in the Interview, but also gives them a good chance to improve their reading skills and enrich their vocabulary. Provided that one of the books suits your class's interests and attitudes, one should be recommended and discussed regularly in class. Written work should also be set on the particular book chosen.

The Teacher's Book

This Teacher's Book contains briefly-expressed ideas on how to handle the various kinds of exercises, together with ideas for discussion, answer keys and transcripts. It is recommended that the teaching notes be checked through before the lesson, so that teachers are prepared for any eventuality that may arise and can take appropriate action.

The notes for the first unit are more comprehensive than those for later units in order to explain and justify the methods underlying each kind of exercise. The notes for units 17 and 18 contain a lot of exam tips for students.

A few more points

If you have not taught a Proficiency class before, you can find out more about the exam itself by looking at unit 18 and at the practice tests in *Cambridge Proficiency Examination Practice 1* (CUP, 1984). You should also study the current examination Regulations, obtainable free of charge from your Local Examinations Secretary, which also includes the list of books for Prescribed Reading.

If your students will be taking the Listening and Interview papers some weeks before they take the written papers, make sure that you schedule a mock listening test and a mock interview some time before they reach the last unit in the book, perhaps using exercises 18.6 and 18.7.

It's a sad fact that students at this level find it difficult to appreciate that they are making progress: you can give them encouragement by keeping a permanent record of their work throughout the course. Each student's work can be sub-categorised into the different skills that will be assessed in the exam: vocabulary, composition writing, reading comprehension, use of English, listening comprehension and speaking skills (communicative ability, grammatical accuracy and pronunciation). These individual 'profiles' can be kept up to date and shown to students from time to time, so that they can see what improvements they have made and also what aspects of their English they still need to work on. Make sure they realise that the purpose of this is to help, not intimidate them!

1 Adventure

1.1 Vocabulary

A The first part of the exercise is a warm-up discussion, to be done as a class or with students working in groups of four or more. Encourage students to think of suitable words to describe explorers. Depending on your attitude an adventurer is the kind of person who is: bold, courageous, fearless, reckless, dashing, impetuous, determined, egotistical, rash, etc.

B After checking students' understanding of the vocabulary, get them to do the exercise in pairs (or groups of three). Afterwards help them to remember the words by reading the incomplete sentences aloud and getting them to call out the missing words, without looking at their books, like this:
Teacher: Going round the world in a hot-air balloon was a fantastic . . .
Students: Achievement!
    Alternatively, if this kind of exercise seems daunting, you could go through it all *before* students work on it in pairs – but they should *not* make notes at this stage, just try to remember any new vocabulary they come across. Only later should they write things down, when working in pairs.

C In pairs again. Students who finish quickly can be asked to help the ones who are making heavy weather of the exercise. Afterwards, get the class to call out the missing words as you read the sentences aloud. They should not be looking at their books, but should try to remember the words:
Teacher: The view from the peak was . . .
Students: Absolutely breathtaking!
or ask them questions requiring similar answers, like this:
Teacher: What was the view from the peak like?
Students: It was absolutely breathtaking!

Answers

1 foolhardy   2 achievement   3 lose heart
4 companionship   5 tempting fate
6 jeopardised   7 modesty   8 determination   9 hardships
10 hair-raising   11 going round in circles   12 safe and sound

11

13 leader   14 summit   15 glacier   16 narrow
17 breathtaking   18 hang-glider   19 parachute   20 oasis
21 rapids (*or* ravine)   22 overboard   23 colonies
24 armchair
If students come up with any plausible alternatives to the model
answers above, be prepared to accept them. For example, answers 1 and
5 are interchangeable and answer 17 could be, more prosaically,
'beautiful'.

1.2 Brazilian Adventure   *Reading*

Background   To help students to appreciate the passage, the
following background information may be helpful
and interesting. You should summarise it or abridge it according to your
class's tastes:

Peter Fleming was the brother of Ian Fleming, creator of James Bond.
Brazilian Adventure, published in 1933, describes in hilarious detail the
writer's experiences of an expedition to the Brazilian jungle, which he joined
after answering this advertisement in *The Times*:

> EXPLORING and sporting expedition,
> under experienced guidance, leaving
> England June, to explore rivers Cen-
> tral Brazil, if possible ascertain fate
> Colonel Fawcett; abundance game,
> big and small; exceptional fishing;
> ROOM TWO MORE GUNS; highest
> references expected and given.—
> Write Box X, *The Times* E.C.4.

Peter Fleming's other books include *One's Company*, an exciting account of
a journey through China in 1933.

A   After reading the passage (which could have been set as homework),
students should do the exercise in pairs or groups of three. Pairs who
finish quickly can move on to section B. To answer some of the questions,
students will need to 'read between the lines' – perhaps warn them about
this.

Answers   2 intrepid (ie courageous)   3 actors
4 understatement   5 one   6 contradictory
7 worried, apprehensive   8 little   9 has done everything, has had
many adventures and jobs   10 Major Pingle   11 their Organiser
12 several   13 no   14 preparations, arrangements   15 fiasco
(though probably not a disaster)

B   These questions are for discussion as a class or in groups.
The tone: ironical, deadpan, humorous, amusing?

Students should justify their answers to the second question by referring to the style or content of the passage.

Finally, if this hasn't become clear implicitly, explain that the aim of this exercise has been to help students to understand the passage and *also* to appreciate it as a piece of effective writing. In the passages that are used in later units, the same aims are pursued: to understand *and* to appreciate or enjoy the writing.

1.3 Everest in Winter
Reading

Background This report, one of a series from Joe Tasker, who was a professional mountaineer not a journalist, appeared in 1980. Three years later Joe Tasker and another climber died while making an attempt to climb the north-east ridge of Everest. (Perhaps don't mention this until students have done the exercise.)

Students should find the answers by working together in pairs.

Answers

1 high winds   2 John Porter   3 numbness in the extremities
4 some Japanese climbers   5 not part of Tasker's report   6 snow cave in crevasse 1,000 ft above Camp II   7 in a snow cave along an easy, windswept ridge at 25,000 feet   8 permit expires 15 February
9 four   10 strong winds
The tone: matter-of-fact, unemotional, straightforward

Discussion ideas What do you think of mountaineers like Joe Tasker? Do you admire them or what? Have you ever been up a high mountain? What was it like? What is the attraction of being high up in the mountains: walking, climbing or ski-ing?

1.4 Prepositions
Use of English

If the exercise seems daunting to your students, you can make it less so by reading the whole text aloud to them complete with all the prepositions – this will make the whole thing 'make sense' to them to start with. Then, working in pairs, they should do the exercise and put in all the missing prepositions. Point out that several variations are possible.

Answers 1 without   2 at   3 over (*or* above)
4 around (*or* in front of *or* before)   5 in

6 with   7 to (*or* towards)   8 in   9 of   10 in (*or* during)
11 through   12 during   13 by   14 within   15 in
16 into   17 On   18 at   19 over (*or* nearly)   20 in
21 including   22 During   23 for   24 around   25 For
26 On (*or* During)   27 without   28 Unlike   29 for   30 like

---

1.5 Idioms with TAKE   *Use of English*

The odd-numbered units in this book each contain an exercise of this type,
exploring phrasal verbs and idiomatic expressions. Naturally, only a
selection of 'Proficiency-level' expressions appears in each exercise, and
students will need to be familiar with other more common idioms.

The exercise can be done in pairs. Afterwards get students to call out the
idioms as you 'test' them on the exercise, like this:
Teacher: He couldn't stop looking at the crocodile?
Class: He couldn't take his eyes off the crocodile.
or
Teacher: Why did the climbers get very wet?
Class: A thunderstorm took them by surprise.

Answers

2   The members of the party took it in turns to steer the boat.
3   They had to take their vehicles to pieces to get them across the gorge.
4   The climbers were taken by surprise by a thunderstorm and got very
    wet.
5   Bob agreed to take on the leadership of the expedition.
6   The world was taken in by his fantastic story of having got to the Pole
    alone.
7   He took up his story after a pause for questions and refreshments.
8   That takes me back to the time I climbed to the top of Mount Fuji.
9   He couldn't take his eyes off the crocodile's jaws.
10 They took it for granted that someone would pick up their signals and
    come to their aid.

1.6 The white man in   *Questions and summary*
Africa

Background   Basil Davidson is an eminent expert on the history
                      of Africa. The book from which the extract comes
is based on a fascinating TV series, broadcast in 1984. He has written over
30 books on Africa, published in 22 countries.

The purpose of this exercise is to lead students towards answering the kinds of questions set in the last part of the Proficiency Use of English paper. This is why the questions should be answered in writing. First, however, students should discuss how they are going to answer, working in groups or pairs. The actual writing may be best set as homework.

The answers to these Questions and summary exercises are given in note form, though students are of course expected to write coherent grammatical sentences, where appropriate. Questions on vocabulary should be answered by working out meanings from context – not by copying definitions from a dictionary.

Answers

1 standpoint – point of view   missionaries – people who attempted to convert the Africans to Christianity   successor – the organisation that took over the Association's dealings   popular craze – fashionable pursuit   slave – person who is owned by another person
2 disapproving
3 forgetting the real origins of the slave trade
4 ironical
5 quotation from previous paragraph
6 slave trade
7 to establish monopoly of trade on land;
to stop Africans from participating in this trade;
as a base for colonising the mainland

1.7   Safety in the hills   *Listening*

Students will probably need to hear the recording at least twice to get all the answers. Follow the steps suggested in the Student's Book, but perhaps get them to listen to the recording once through to get the gist before they fill in the missing information.

Alternatively, to give time for students to become accustomed to the voices, play the first 30 seconds or so of the recording before you rewind it and then play the whole thing without interruption.

The recording is part of a radio broadcast.

Answers

1 four people
2 bad weather   weather forecasts
3 time   darkness
4 slowest   poor visibility
5 map   compass   direction

6 waterproof
7 walking boots   jeans   sandals
8 set out   where   what time   back   safe arrival

Transcript

Presenter: Well, in case all this talk about mountaineering and the open-air life tempts you to go out on the hills yourself, here's some timely advice on how not to run the kind of risks that can get you into trouble – from Tim Barrow. Tim, what advice would you give?

Tim: Well, above all you've got to use your common sense and not try to do what you're not trained to do. First of all, for example, you shouldn't set out into the hills by yourself. That's the worst thing you can do. It's best to have at least four people in the party, so that . . er . . two can go for help if someone is injured . . er . . while the third person stays with the person who's hurt.

Presenter: Oh, that sounds as if you expect everyone to hurt themselves, Tim?

Tim: Haha, no. No, of course not . . er . . but you've got to be careful and if you take precautions then you're going to enjoy your . . your walking. You should . . um . . expect, for example, bad weather . . um . . you shouldn't rely on the accuracy of weather forecasts, because the . . things can change very very quickly. Um . . you give yourself plenty of time to . . to get where you're going to go . . er . . and especially, you know, to take into account darkness so that it doesn't catch you up and leave you still out . . out in the hills. Um . . don't leave anyone behind. You should walk . . er . . as slowly as the slowest walker. Er . . now if the visibility does get bad, due to fog or low-lying cloud,

the best thing is not to go on walking – stop and wait for it to get better . . er . . otherwise you might walk over a precipice or something horrendous like that. Um . . you need to take – most important this – a map and compass, because it can be disastrous if you try and follow your nose and expect your sense of direction to get you . . er . . anywhere.

Presenter: Yes, and . . er . . how about clothes and . . and equipment?

Tim: Well, crucial. Um . . you've got to be . . you've got to take precautions, be prepared for the wet, even if when you start out it looks warm and . . and sunny. Um . . you can't . . you just can't assume that it's going to stay that way . . er . . so take warm clothes and waterproof ones at that. Er . . next, you should take proper walking boots . . er . . not sandals, things like that, and not jeans, which . . er . .

Presenter: Oh.

Tim: Yes, I know, lots of people wear jeans but . . um . . they just don't protect you against the . . the wind or the . . or the rain. Um . . another important thing: before you set out, you should actually let people know . . er . . where you're going and what time you'll be back. Um . . then if you do get into difficulties you . . you've got a chance of being rescued. And very important when you do get back to report that you've arrived safely back, otherwise everyone will be terribly worried that . . that . . that's very important.

Presenter: Yes. Well, that's good advice. Thanks, Tim.

(Time: 2 minutes 40 seconds)

16

Which of the precautions suggested would you take (and not take) if you were going for a walk in the mountains? Does it make any difference if it's winter or summer? Or if you're in northern Britain or in your own country?

1.8   A Japanese adventurer   *Listening*

Again, follow the steps suggested in the Student's Book, with a preliminary 30-second playing to get used to the voices if necessary.
The recording is part of a radio broadcast.

Answers

Ascents: 1964   1970   1970 (North America)   1968 (South America)   1966 (Africa)   Mt Jaja ✕
Solo journeys: 1968 raft   1979 (2,250 km)   1974–6 (12,000 km)
1978   across the Pacific ✕   across Antarctica ✕

Transcript

Presenter: . . one of the most remarkable of all the present-day adventurers is the Japanese, Naomi Uemura. Bob McArthur has been looking at his career. Bob?
Bob: Yes . . er . . that's right, Sue. Well . . er . . Mr Uemura is . . er . . certainly a remarkable man. Er . . in his life he's achieved a . . a number of 'firsts' for the record books . . um . . but to begin with here's a . . a short biography. He was born in 1941, he was the youngest of seven children . . ah . . and in university he . . um . . he achieved a degree in agriculture, but . . er . . at the same time I suppose he . . he developed his taste for climbing mountains, especially alone. Er . . after he got his degree, he travelled to America with only $100 in his pocket. Er . . anyway, he eventually made his way to Europe and . . er . . first of all he climbed Mount . . Mont Blanc . . er . . and this is despite the fact that he spoke very little English and no French at all – that was back in 1964. Um . . the next year he joined the

Japanese expedition to the Himalayas – this was the famous ascent of the Cho Oyu and in the years that followed he wandered around the world with . . er . . little money and he just, apparently, looked for bigger mountains to climb. In 1966 he . . er . . he found himself in Africa, where he climbed Mt Kilimanjaro and Mt Kenya and the next year he climbed . . er . . Mt Sanford in Alaska. And the year after that he was down in Argentina and . . er . . climbed the Ac . . the . . er – sorry, I'm having a little trouble with my paper here – the Aconcagua, which is the highest mountain in the Andes. Er . . the same year he floated on a wooden raft down the Amazon from its source to the mouth of the river, which I think's incredible.
Presenter: Yes, indeed, and . . er . . what . . what did he do next? What happened after that?
Bob: Well, next was the . . he . . his famous . . his first ascent of . . er . . Everest. Er . . Uemura joined the Japanese expedition, which was . .

they were making a reconnaissance of the South-West Face – that was in '69. Er . . he returned the next year and that was the year that the expedition split in two: one . . er . . one group attempted to . . er . . to climb the difficult South-West Face and the other . . er . . climbed the South Col route, which was . . er . . easier and . . er . . Uemura joined the latter group. Er . . and as you may know the members of the South-West Face party didn't make it but the . . er . . the South Col party eventually did. Um . . anyway, the same year he travelled to Alaska again to climb Mt McKinley and so this made Aemura . . Uemura, sorry . . the first man to get to the highest point of five different continents.

Presenter: Yes. Um . . wasn't he a member of . . of that ill-fated i . . international Everest exhib . . expedition in . . er . . 1971? Um . . the . . the one that failed because of all those arguments . . er . . that happened between all the . . all the members of the group?

Bob: That's . . that's right yes, but they didn't . . they failed also because the weather was . . was pretty bad. Um . . Uemura and his partner were . . er . . for some reason had to carry the supplies for the British pair . . er . . who insisted that . . er . . they could . . that they would do all the exciting climbing for themselves, so obviously there was a bit of resentment there.

Presenter: Yes, no doubt that . . that must have made him quite determined to . . er . . just concentrate on . . on solo expeditions after that . . that experience?

Bob: Yes apparently, yeah. Well, I know that he . . he's gone solo since then. Er . . in 1974 he . . he set off in . . in the middle of winter to cross the North American continent from Greenland to the Bering Straits by dog sled, which was an incredible idea in

(Time: 5 minutes)

the first place – that's a distance of 12,000 kilometres. And . . er . . of course this was totally by himself, the only company he had were . . er . . his dogs. Um . . apparently he met people on the way but . . er . . you know he . . he was doing it all himself . . er . . and he travelled in the winter and in the summer he rested and it took him two years. Eventually he got to the Pacific in '76. Must have got a lot of reading done during the summer! Um . . anyway, two years later . . um . . he found sponsors to finance a solo expedition to the North Pole. Supplies were flown in by . . by plane and he maintained radio contact with his sponsors but he was completely alone out there. Er . . he was attacked by a polar bear, he nearly fell through the ice . . er . . it was incredible but apparently he . . er . . he got from the northern part of Canada to the . . er . . to the North Pole in 54 days. And the next year, not content with that, he crossed the entire Greenland ice cap, which is 2,250 kilometres and it . . er . . it's . . mo . . part of it's . . some of the most bleakest terrain in the world.

Presenter: Yes, yes, and his dream is . . is to cross the Antarctic continent a . . alone, isn't it?

Bob: Yes, yes, he's been preparing . . er . . to try it. It's never been done before, but . . er . . you know, if anyone can do it I imagine he can – he's certainly determined and he doesn't seem to mind the . . er . . the loneliness. A . . apparently he is a . . a happily married family man, I don't know how he manages that, but . . er . . anyway if he can get permission and . . and financial backing, there's really nothing to stop them. I . . er . . I guess after he does that there won't be anything left for him to do.

Presenter: Well, we'll see. Bob McArthur, thank you very much.

Bob: It's all right.

18

Discussion ideas How would you feel if you were Uemura's wife?
Do you admire his feats? Would you like to
accomplish a 'first' for the record books? What's your opinion about
record books (like the *Guinness Book of Records*) and the information they
contain?

1.9 Dangerous pursuits *Picture conversation*

Put students into pairs. One should look at communication activity 1 at the
end of the Student's Book (on page 256), the other at activity 37 (on page
280). Activity 1 has a photo of a young woman climbing a precipice, activity
37 shows a couple watching a strangely-attired man preparing for a flight in
(on?) his hang-glider.

The idea of the activity is to get students to use the questions to bridge the
'information gap'. Only at the very end are they allowed to see each other's
pictures.

Listen in to each group and suggest to them what are the main areas of
improvement they should aim for.

1.10 Around the world *Communication activity*

Again in pairs. Activity 7 gives information about the first half of Naomi
James's solo round-the-world yacht voyage, activity 39 has information
about the second half. The partners have to find out each other's
information. (Naomi James was the first woman to accomplish this feat.)

Suggest to each group you listen to what areas of improvement you think
they should concentrate on.

1.11 Writing a narrative *Composition*

Follow the steps suggested in the Student's Book.

Draw students' attention to the need for A GOOD INTRODUCTION in a
narrative. Setting the scene and catching the reader's attention is vital. Does
the first part of the example given in the Student's Book do this effectively?
If not, how could it be done better to introduce the story? Is it better to
explain what you're going to write about at the start, or to let the reader do
some work to find out what you want to say? Look at some examples of
introductory paragraphs among the narrative passages in this book. After
the compositions have been done as homework (step 2), compare the
openings of them all and discuss which are the more effective ones.

(In every unit there will be a different aspect of composition writing to draw students' attention to. This is left to the teacher to introduce, as the amount of detail or explanation required will vary from class to class.)

Treat this and the next few compositions as a 'diagnosis' of each student's composition-writing. What are the major points each should concentrate on improving?

Make sure everyone understands your system of marking written work and the meaning of the symbols you use. At this level there's no point in your correcting every little mistake that students have made – it's better for them to locate and correct their own mistakes, with some guidance in the form of symbols in the margin, like these:

A cross (**X**) in the margin is enough to indicate that somewhere in the line there is some kind of mistake that should be corrected. Other symbols can be used in the margin to indicate particular kinds of mistakes in, for example: grammar (**G**), vocabulary (**V**), spelling (**Sp**), word order (**WO**), punctuation (**P**) or – very important at this level – inappropriate style (**ST**). A question mark (**?**) in the margin can show that an idea has not been expressed clearly and a tick (✓) is a nice way of showing that an idea has been expressed particularly effectively or amusingly.

You may have your own views on whether or not to award a mark for each composition – if you do, allow scope in your system for students to see an improvement over the months: it's pretty discouraging if you're still getting the same mark even at the end of the course! Instead, you may prefer to write a few appreciative and helpfully critical comments.

When you mark each composition, pay particular attention to the aspect of writing you have highlighted in the unit. In this unit, for example, make sure that each student has written a good introduction to the narrative. Students can help each other a lot here, by evaluating and criticising each other's compositions. Surprisingly, if students know that a colleague is going to read their work, they tend to take a lot more care over it than if it's 'only' the teacher who's going to see it!

2 Language

(You might perhaps begin by doing listening exercise 2.7 to start the ball rolling – especially if the class found it hard to get started on the first vocabulary exercise.)

2.1 Vocabulary

The four parts of the exercise should be done by students working together in pairs or groups of three, with a pause between each part for questions and for you to 'test' students by reading out the incomplete sentences (or rephrasing them as questions) while the class calls out the missing words without looking at their notes.

The purpose of section C is to look at different words that can be used in the same context. Make sure students consider the meanings of the *in*correct answers as well.

A 2 synonyms   3 antonyms   4 jargon   5 slang   6 Received Pronunciation   7 irony   8 sarcasm   9 proverbs   10 cliché

B : colon   ! exclamation mark   - hyphen   — dash
" " inverted commas (*or* quotation marks)   * asterisk
( ) brackets (*or* parentheses)   / stroke (*or* oblique)
's apostrophe 's'

C 12 mumbling, murmuring, muttering   13 jot, note, scribble
14 glance at, scan, skim   15 chuckling, grinning, sniggering
16 frown, scowl, sneer   17 scream, shriek, yell   18 imply, intimate, suggest   19 attitude, expression, tone   20 expression, phrase, idiom

D ie – that is   pp – page numbers   NB – note carefully
cf – compare   qv – see elsewhere   © – copyright   ff – the following pages   ibid – in the book already referred to

2.2   Attitudes to language   *Reading*

<u>*Background*</u>   Anthony Burgess is a well-known novelist, author
of *A Clockwork Orange* and *Earthly Powers*. The
book from which this passage is taken is a lay person's guide to
linguistics, published in 1975.

The exercise is best done in pairs, after having been read through perhaps as
homework.
   The theme of the discussion questions at the end is taken up in Listening
exercise 2.7 and in the Composition exercise at the end of this unit.

<u>*Answers*</u>

1 true	2 false	3 false	4 false
5 false	6 true	7 false	8 true

9 true	10 true	11 false	12 true	13 true	14 true

2.3   This book...   *Reading*

This exercise concentrates on style. Suggested answers are given to the
questions posed, but these are tentative rather than authoritative. A reader's
reactions to a piece of writing are personal, unpredictable and often
surprising – make sure, therefore, that everyone has understood the extracts
and hasn't got hold of the wrong end of the stick.

Tentative answers

1 Extract A a) an academic, no personal information given
               b) to provide a scholarly document
               c) experts in or students of the writer's field
   Extract B a) earnest, sincere poet
               b) to move, influence, inspire the reader
               c) people who will share the poet's attitudes
   Extract C a) ??
               b) to interest, entertain and educate
               c) students of English, but not elementary ones
2 'general perspective'; 'considerations of interpretation'; 'with which I
   shall be concerned' etc.
3 'my poems shine in your eye'; 'they look from your walls'; 'lurk on your
   shelves'; 'to become a weapon', etc.
4 'will help you to'; 'These three requirements are kept in mind
   throughout'. (But much of this extract is not pragmatic – it's more like a

piece of advertising copy: 'often entertaining, sometimes challenging, frequently . . . ,' etc.)
5 B because it catches the imagination and can be read over and over with increasing pleasure.

Discussion ideas   Do you always read the introduction to a book carefully? Why (not)? A non-fiction book contains a lot of useful information in its contents, chapter headings and index – what use can you make of these when approaching the book for the first time? How useful is the 'blurb' on the back cover?

2.4 Reporting speech   *Use of English*

Spend time on both parts of the exercise – ask for suggestions on *who* might have said each utterance and *in what situation* it might have been said.
    (Reported speech is practised again in 6.5 and 12.4.)

Suggested answers

2 She advised me not to start giggling during the interview.
3 He dissuaded me from writing it all out in longhand (and told me to use a typewriter).
4 She warned me not to boast about my command of English.
5 He advised me to listen to recordings of different English accents.
6 She persuaded me to type the letter for her.
7 He accused me of stealing his dictionary.
8 She forgave me for being rude to her.
9 He apologised for breaking my fountain pen.
10 She allowed me to use her typewriter.
(There are many possible variations to the suggested answers above – be prepared to accept any that are plausible and accurately written.)

2.5 Verbs followed by *ing, to . . .*   *Use of English*
and *that . . .*

Both the matching exercise and the gap-filling should be done by students working together in pairs. Allow time for questions and discussion at the end of each part.

A to call someone on the phone
to contact someone by phone/by post
to drop someone a line
to get through to someone on the phone
to give someone a ring

to keep in touch with
someone
to reply to a letter
to tell someone a story
to write someone a letter

B 2 in contacting him
3 to replying to
4 to send him
5 tell the story
6 to reply to

7 to calling people
8 in getting through to her
9 to drop me
10 giving me

2.6 Hello, darling   *Questions and summary*

Answers

1 not normally appropriate; not suitable for the situation
2 'Hello, darling' and 'hello, dear' to wife; 'Hello, dear' and 'Hello, darling' old lady to pussy-cat(??); 'Dear reader' author to reader(?); 'Dear Sir' to Commissioner of Taxes; 'Hello, dear' to neighbour's wife(?)
3 its vast intricate code (ie system of syntax or grammar)
4 how it works in different situations
5 Writing is more organised and artificial than spontaneous speech and has little regard for changing external circumstances
6 Speech: spontaneous, precarious
Writing: careful, elaborated, edited, tidied
7 He worked in Adelaide and in Hampstead; he lived with his family in Adelaide ('our house'); he works at home; the first draft of the book was written in Adelaide, commented on by two editors and rewritten six months later in Hampstead

Discussion ideas   Think of some more examples of inappropriate language being used incongruously. For language to be appropriate, what conditions must be fulfilled?

2.7 Speaking with an accent   *Listening*

Students may need to hear the recording twice to get all the answers. Allow time for pairs to compare their answers between the two playings.

The recording is a conversation between friends. Ann, who claims that her accent is RP, has a slight North of England accent in fact.

Answers

1 are no longer looked down on
2 more different accents than the USA
3 whether different social classes used different pronunciations
4 because they would have tried to use the 'best' pronunciation
5 common
6 did get laughed at because of their Southern accents
7 out of place
8 Teachers used RP
   RP was used by the BBC
   A standard is needed to avoid confusion

Transcript

Ann: . . . you know, I think it's a great shame the way regional accents seem to be dying out in England, don't you?

Ken: Oh, I don't think they are. In fact, I think there's been a bit of a revival in . . you know, recently. I mean, it may be true of dialects, but not accents. Er . . in fact a regional accent is socially acceptable in all walks of life now, I think. Think of the BBC: I mean, they have announcers and presenters with Scots accents . . er . . one of its political reporters has a strong Northern Ireland accent.

Ann: Yeah, you can't understand him very well, can you? Haha.

Kerry: No, seriously, I think it's . . it's wonderful. There's such an enormous range of accents in your country. You know, Britain is . . is, I don't know, about a sixteenth the size of the States but it's got more variety, more vocal variety than . . than . . .

Ann: You know, all Americans sound the same to me. I mean . . .

Kerry: How do you mean?

Ann: Well, they all pronounce 'r' at the end of every word.

Kerry: No, that's not true.

Ken: Well, I don't know if that's true or not, but I mean many British speakers do the same: you think of the . . the West Country burr and . . and in Scotland there's a slight audible 'rr' at the end of . . of words.

Kerry: Oh, that . . that reminds me. I heard about this . . er . . strange experiment they did in New York City. Um . . linguists wanted to find out if lower-class and middle-class people pronounced that 'r' sound differently. So they chose these three department stores in New York and one was a high status, and one was medium status, one was low status. And . . er . . they found out what departments were on . . um . . a particular floor. For instance, they went around asking all the assistants 'Where's the toy department?' or the bookstore or whatever and they were all on the fourth floor. And they . . so the . . the answer they got was always 'Fourth floor', 'Fourth floor'.

Ken: Haha. Like that! Oh, the trouble is when you ask someone to pronounce something they affect a high status pronunciation, thinking that's the correct way to talk, I suppose. Um . . certainly in the UK the people with strongest accents are working-class, I think. As .. as in the United States?

Kerry: I never thought about that.

Ann: You .. you know what's strange is the way different sorts of accents .. different sorts of sounds make people .. make you assume that people are slightly slow-witted or unintelligent – like, you know, West country accents or Suffolk accents, because it .. it's slow, you know, slow rural accent. But an urban accent, like London or Liverpool just makes you sound un-educated. I mean, I know it's pre-judice but it .. it's got something to do with what .. with what Ken's saying. But what I was trying to say, is .. is this the same in North America?

Kerry: Er .. yeah, probably to a .. to a lesser extent, I think. There's a .. there's a .. there is a working class accent in .. er .. in New York City and Chicago pretty well any city but especially the big cities . . .

Ken: So the Bronx . . .

Kerry: That's right, people talk like that and .. and it doesn't necessarily, you know, mean anything except that . . .

Ann: Do you have a rural accent the same?

Kerry: Well, there . . . Yes, there are rural accents. I mean, you know, there's .. you've probably heard, you know, Hillbillies in the South or, you know, in the Mid-West, but it's funny because a lot of the American Presi-dents came from the South, like John-son and Carter. And they get made fun of really, because of their accents too.

Ken: Yes . . . What happened to me when I was in the States is people kept asking me to talk because they liked to listen to a British accent. I suppose it sounded sort of quaint to them. Wait-resses in restaurants particularly.

Kerry: 'Gee, I just love your British accent!'

Ken: 'Your British accent', yeah!

Ann: Mind you, an accent like yours or mine .. er .. RP they call it, don't they, can be a handicap in some situations in this country. I mean, people think you're stuck-up or .. or trying to be superior.

Ken: Mm, yes. But in general RP has high prestige.

Kerry: But it .. it's funny because RP has .. as you call it is .. is only spoken by a .. a tiny minority of people .. er .. er .. of people who speak English as their first language. So why is it, tell me, that .. that it's become a model for .. for almost all .. well, every foreigner learning the language?

Ken: Ah, yes. Mainly in Europe – it's not so much in Asia and Latin Amer-ica. But I think it has to do with the prestige of RP in .. in the UK and the way it was the BBC accent for so long – you know, BBC spans the world and .. and don't forget, RP 'the accent of educated, middle-class Southern Bri-tain' was also the accent of teachers.

Ann: Yeah, that's true. And also .. er .. I mean, there has got to be some sort of standard, even if it's an artificial one. Otherwise people get confused and there's no sort of norm to stick to, is there? I mean, I .. I've never met a foreigner that doesn't speak with an accent, but a .. a national one, rather than a regional one and .. and that's sometimes really enchanting and I don't think we'd want to change that . . .

(Time: 4 minutes)

Discussion ideas

Where is the 'best' accent of your own language spoken? Is there a special standard accent used on TV or taught to foreigners? Which foreign accents do you find 'enchanting' or 'disagreeable'?

2.8 Who's talking?   *Listening*

Pause the tape after each monologue for pairs to discuss their answers before they hear the next one. The answers given below are suggestions and plausible variations should be accepted if they can be justified.

The recording consists of five monologues.

Answers

1   angry; at home
2   her husband (or older child?)
3   books or papers? (toys??)
4   the children (from school) or some people (from the station?)
5   indifferent or defiant?
6   wants to avoid conflict?

7   a female stranger
8   he mistakes her for a well-known TV actress
9   TV stars or characters in TV programmes
10 doesn't want to get involved? aloof?

11 teacher of English
12 students; the English language
13 one or possibly two

14 busybody
15 child (little girl?)
16 flowers
17 cry
18 intimidated?

19 factory manager
20 reporters
21 pollution or radioactive leak
22 ?

Transcript

FIRST SPEAKER: . . . Oh, but look! They're all over the place! Oh, I'm fed up with it, really I am. If I've told you once, I've told you a thousand times. Why should I have to do it for you? You're the one who put them there and they're yours not mine. Oh yes, I know, you're 'going to do it later'. If I had a pound for every time I've heard that excuse, I'd be a millionaire. Look, I've got better things to do. Don't look like that, of course it matters, it's symptomatic of your whole attitude. Oh God, it's almost time to pick them up now and I've got nothing done at all this afternoon, thanks to you . Yes, it is your fault and don't pretend it's not and they're just as bad. They think

27

if you can get away with it, so can they. It's just not fair. I'm warning you, if you don't make an effort to . . .

SECOND SPEAKER: . . .er . . (*cough*) . . excuse me, aren't you . . er . . . . Oh no, of course you're not. Sorry. Silly of me. It's just that from the side and in this light . . erm . . but now I can see I was wrong. A . . and you're quite a bit taller too, I can see that. Sorry again. Has . . er . . anyone ever made that mistake before, I wonder? The . . er . . no, I suppose not. Don't you? Oh, you know, Jane . . Jane . . er . . something. I can't remember her other name. You know, the one who was in that sitcom . . er . . she was the daughter and Terry Scott was the father. Er . . no, no, no, not Terry Scott, that other chap. The . . the one with the stutter. Um . . oh, Terry something anyway. Oh, and the mother was whatsername, that blonde actress – you know, the one who died just recently. Wo . . they said it was accidental, but I have my doubts between the two of us. Haha. Anyway, this . . this Jane something was in that Indian thing too – well, you must have seen that! The . . the . . she was the . . the sister of . . um . . oh . . .

THIRD SPEAKER: . . . well, you see, initially it all boils down to phonology. You see, there's a tendency for some of them to assume that it's syllable-timed, just like theirs, and of course, it's not. And this leads them into all sorts of difficulties. I mean, that doesn't stop them being mutually intelligible as they share the same misconceptions but to the untrained ear it sounds like gibberish. Funnily enough, poor articulation hardly ever seems as great a handicap. I suppose it's easier for an interlocutor to adjust. And then of course everyone does

have syntactical problems at first but in later years, when the basic items have been mastered, they reach a sort of plateau, where they still have to extend their lexical range and master the more complex rules of use and usage but find that they seem to have stopped making the kind of silly . . .

FOURTH SPEAKER: . . . no, I don't think so. No, you shouldn't. I know there are lots of them but it's wrong. What if everybody did it? There'd be none left, would there? And you've got so many. It must have taken you ages to get all those. No, you can't go round and put them all back where you got them, you just . . it can't be done. No, don't give them to me either. The important thing is not to do it again. They're here for everyone to enjoy, don't you understand? How would you like it if someone came into your garden and started taking yours? You're a very, very . . . Oh, no, no, don't get so upset. There . . there's no need to . . . Oh, dear, I . . look, I didn't mean to make you . . .

FIFTH SPEAKER: No . . . there's absolutely no truth in the rumour, none whatsoever. I've been assured by my staff, that every possible precaution is routinely taken and nothing like that could possibly have happened. The odds against it happening are literally thousands to one. So you see it couldn't have happened. However, to set the public's mind to rest, the whole area is to be closed to visitors for a period of ten days while tests are made, thorough scientific tests by our own team of experts. But, as I said, there is absolutely no danger to the public at this moment in time. Nor is there any likelihood in the future of any . . .

(Time: 4 minutes 35 seconds)

What were the 'clues' that helped you to answer
the questions? What can you find out from a
speaker's tone of voice? Or from a speaker's accent?

2.9 Blurbs   *Pronunciation*

Student A has an extract from the back cover of the *Longman Dictionary of
Contemporary English* (in activity 2); student B has an extract from the
cover of the *Oxford Advanced Learner's Dictionary* (in activity 40).
 The purpose of this exercise is to focus students' attention on their
pronunciation – particularly their stress and intonation. Each has both the
original version of their extract and an 'easy-to-read' version with stressed
syllables marked and long sentences divided into 'breath-sized chunks'.
After listening to students' pronunciation, give advice on what they need to
improve. They don't need to sound like professional radio announcers, but
they do need to be able to speak clearly and without too strong a foreign
accent!
 Which extract is more persuasive? Which dictionary sounds better?

2.10 Meanings of words   *Communication activity*

One student has definitions of half the words shown (in activity 5), the other
definitions of the other half (in activity 38). Make sure they paraphrase the
information using their own words and do *not* simply read their
information aloud.
 As you listen to the pairs at work, note down any general points for
improvement that you want to announce at the end of the activity.

2.11 Writing a short report   *Composition*

The exercise should begin with students making notes in answer to the
questions, preferably alone. Then they should explain their ideas to a
partner before writing the report as homework.
 Draw students' attention to the need for USING PARAGRAPHS in an effective
manner. When does one begin a new paragraph in a composition? What is
the purpose of a paragraph? What is the effect of having paragraphs that are
very long? Or very short? Take a look at some of the discursive passages in
this book to see how the system of paragraphs works. In marking the
completed reports pay particular attention to the use of paragraphs, and
remind students of this when you hand back the marked work.

3 People

(Perhaps begin with listening exercise 3.8.)

3.1 Vocabulary

The five parts of the exercise are best done in pairs, though to start things off as a class, you might like to do section E all together as a class, preferably with extra photos of other people (collected from magazines – or photos of the class's friends and relations, perhaps?).

Answers

A 1 step-father (*or* step-brother *or* step-sister)   2 half-brother
3 maternal   4 guardian   5 foster

B 6 make friends with   7 row (*or* argument *or* quarrel) with
8 living together   9 arranged   10 divorced from

C conceited – modest   deceitful – honest, frank   lazy – industrious,
hard-working   malicious – kind-hearted, well-meaning   mean –
generous, kind   narrow-minded – broad-minded, unprejudiced
secretive – open, candid   sullen – cheerful, jolly   solitary –
gregarious, sociable   touchy – easy-going, nonchalant

D as blind as a bat   as hard as nails
as deaf as a post   as quiet as a mouse
as good as gold   as fit as a fiddle
as thick as two short planks   as mad as a hatter
as cool as a cucumber   as pretty as a picture
(You may like to supplement this list with other similar idioms: as fresh as a daisy, as sober as a judge, as drunk as a lord (*or* skunk), as pleased as Punch, etc.)

E To what extent does everyone agree or disagree with these descriptions?
MAN IN HAT: sixtyish, short-sighted, diffident, meticulous, conventional, dispassionate, set in his ways, diligent, affluent.
BLACK TODDLER: 3-4 years old, baby-faced, soulful, appealing, touching, distrustful, apprehensive, unfortunate, cuddly.

LADY: late 50s, well-groomed, assertive, stern, doesn't suffer fools gladly, pensive, discerning, shrewd, dynamic, quizzical, well-to-do.
MAN WITH CURLY HAIR: late 40s/early 50s, tense, fastidious, solemn, wiry, patient, tenacious, hardy, conscientious, taciturn, careworn.
YOUNG WOMAN: modest, open minded, good-natured, cheerful, good-humoured, natural, unassuming, sincere, guileless, unpretentious.
MAN WITH STRAIGHT HAIR: late 30s, intense, fervent, methodical, sensitive, gentle, aesthetic, restrained, perceptive, erudite, zany.

3.2 Wilt   *Reading*

Background Tom Sharpe is well-known and popular for his comic novels, several of which are about the technical college lecturer, Henry Wilt. Sharpe himself taught for a time at 'the Tech' in Cambridge. The passage is the very first paragraph of the novel, setting the scene for what is to come (murdering his wife? having his own moments of fame and glory?), and whetting the reader's appetite for the fun that is to follow. *Wilt* was first published in 1976.

Answers 1 Mrs Wilt   2 Clem   3 a small house
4 he was a pedigree dog   5 he was not rich
6 daydream   7 losing his wife; becoming rich; becoming powerful and influential   8 he lost them   9 he teaches   10 murder or a contrived accident

Discussion ideas in Student's Book.

3.3 Two short poems   *Reading*

Background Stevie Smith's poems celebrated the pains and hardships of being alone. Stevie Smith herself lived most of her life with an aunt and never married. She died in 1971 at the age of 68.

Christopher Logue, part of whose preface was seen in 2.3, is a respected living poet whose work is easily accessible to the general reader. *Epitaph* was written during his middle age.

Students who are unused to poetry in English (most of them, probably!) may need some help. One indispensable piece of advice is for them to disregard line endings to begin with, and to read the poems as prose, giving full stops and other punctuation their normal prose values. Best of all, read the poems aloud to the class. The questions are quite hard to answer, and should be discussed with the whole class after pairs have attempted to answer them together.

The answers given here are suggestions – your interpretation may differ slightly or considerably.

Answers

1 he drowned, presumably
2 'I was much further out than you thought and not waving but drowning.' 'Oh, no no no, it was too cold always, I was much too far out all my life and not waving but drowning.'
3 'Poor chap, he always loved larking and now he's dead – it must have been too cold for him. His heart gave way.'
4 having fun, playing pranks
5 line 7: the water   line 9 : life
6 line 11: out of control, in despair   line 12: unable to cope
7 not having fun, enjoying himself

8 he had more interests
9 not at all
10 because he has much better ideas (a penny for a shilling is a twelve-fold improvement)
11 he has been in contact with her carefree spirit
12 Perhaps he foresees no further improvements in his life and no new joys in his old age?

Discussion ideas

What is the impact of the two poems on you? Which one impressed you/moved you/depressed you more? What are the similarities between the two poems?

Who do you know who is like the 'drowning man' and the 'old man' in the poems? How are we all like them in some ways? What is the effect of expressing the ideas in poetry, rather than in prose? Do you appreciate poetry yourself, or do you rarely if ever read poetry?

3.4 Articles   *Use of English*

To make the task easier, you could read the whole passage aloud before students try to fill the gaps, supplying all the missing words – this will make the whole thing 'make sense' from the outset.

The passage is the first paragraph of Margaret Drabble's *Jerusalem the Golden* (1967). Margaret Drabble's nine best-selling novels manage to combine good writing with popular appeal. Many of them deal with the problems facing women in modern society, exploring relationships with insight and humour.

Answers (first ones given are the ones used originally by the author)

1 her 2 the 3 the 4 her 5 her 6 Ø (*or* the) 7 Ø
8 the (*or* Ø?) 9 the 10 Ø 11 a (*or* the) 12 Ø 13 Ø
14 the 15 the (*or* Ø?) 16 her 17 an 18 the 19 the
20 Ø 21 a 22 her 23 the 24 an 25 a 26 her
27 her 28 her (*or* Ø??) 29 the 30 her 31 a 32 Ø
33 Ø 34 the 35 Ø (*or* the?) 36 her 37 a

3.5 Idioms with GET
Use of English

Answers

2 This cloudy weather is getting me down.
3 You seem to have got out of bed the wrong side this morning.
   or You seem to have got out of the wrong side of bed this morning.
4 I would like to get this meeting over with as quickly as possible.
5 You won't be able to get (it) through to her what she has to do.
6 We got off on the wrong foot by having a row on our first meeting.
7 Once he starts talking you won't be able to get a word in edgeways.
8 They got their own back by pouring cold water over my head.
9 He gets people's backs up by telling them exactly what's on his mind.
10 Thomas and David get along very well.
11 Don't get me wrong – you seem to have got hold of the wrong end of the stick.
12 One of these days I must get round to replying to all this correspondence.

3.6 Women's rights
Questions and summary

Background *Women's Rights: A Practical Guide* was one of the first comprehensive surveys of the law as it affects women in Britain. The first edition came out in 1974. The authors are a journalist and a solicitor, both activists in the women's movement.

After they have read the passage once through, students should underline the words they'll have to explain in the passage, so that they can see how they fit into their contexts. The answers to all the questions should be discussed before they are written down.

Spend some time looking at how students can *use their own words* to paraphrase the information given in the passage, to avoid direct quotation from it.

Answers

1 oppression – being ruled cruelly   chattels – possessions   legal reprisals – being punished by the law   gains – what they had won maternal deprivation – suffering through the absence of the mother
2 Before 1803: abortion was legal
   Before 1832: women were allowed to vote (in theory at least!)
   Before the 1831–72 Factory Acts: no limits on hours and conditions for women workers; no limits on night working
   Before 1882: married women had no right to own property
   Before 1918: women not allowed to vote
3 During the wars: women needed in factories – allowed to take over men's jobs, given more responsibility; nurseries provided to allow mothers to enter the workforce
   After the wars: men returned from fighting – allowed to reclaim jobs; women returned to low-status jobs or to the home; nurseries closed down; women told children would suffer if they went out to work

Discussion ideas   How does the historical development of women's rights in your country compare with the survey in the article? Do women have adequately protected rights in your country now?

3.7   Sex discrimination   *Listening*

This recording, part of a radio broadcast, takes up the theme of 3.6 and looks at present-day Britain. Before they listen to the recording, students should look at the questions and decide what they *expect* the answers to be, basing these expectations on their own experience and knowledge of their own country's laws.

Answers

Illegal (✗): 1, 3, 7, 8, 11, 14
Not illegal (✓): 2, 4, 5, 6, 9, 10, 12, 13, 15

Discussion ideas   How is the legal situation in your country different? Do you agree with the principles underlying the English laws explained? Should women be protected further, by making, for example, cases 5, 6 or 13 illegal?

Has women's liberation 'had its day'? Is it now time for 'men's liberation'? Should boys and girls receive different educations, according to their 'innate strengths'???

Transcript

Presenter: It's ten years since the Sex Discrimination Act became law and Tessa Blakeway, whose book *Know Your Rights* has just come out in paperback, has been looking at the implications of the Act. Tessa, briefly, what does the Act cover?

Tessa: Well, Tom, there are four main areas, namely: the provision of goods and services, education, employment and training, housing and mortgages.

Presenter: Perhaps you could give us some examples of what is illegal, according to the Act?

Tessa: Yes. Er . . well, let's take the . . the first point, the provision of goods and services. Now, there's a difference between public and private places. It is against the law for women to be refused service in a bar or public house, unless of course she's under age or she's drunk or something like that. Um . . a men-only bar is illegal, but in a private club special rules may be made to exclude women. Or . . or to exclude men, for that matter.

Presenter: I see. Well, let's move on to the second point. What about in schools?

Tessa: Yes. Er . . now again there are differences between single-sex schools and mixed schools. A single-sex school may offer special subjects that another school doesn't. A girls' school may have lessons in domestic science or sewing and none in . . in metalwork or woodwork or mechanics. A mixed school has to offer all pupils the same subjects. For instance . . for example if a boy wants to do typing, or a girl woodwork, he or she has to be allowed to do them if . . if they're in

the school curriculum. Teachers should also encourage girls to continue with their maths and science courses, rather than encourage them to switch to arts subjects. But this of course is up to the individual teachers and is not . . is not covered by the law. Er . . likewise school books are not covered, so if in a book on explorers they describe only male explorers and don't include any female ones, this is not illegal. But of course teachers ideally should refuse to use such books that reinforce the stereotypes. You know the sort of thing: that men are brave, strong, clever and women are submissive and weak and home-loving . . .

Presenter: Housewives, yes. Well, how about the area of employment, then? Advertisements for jobs for example?

Tessa: Ah, now the law's very clear here. There are to be no adverts for, you know the sort of thing, 'Men only need apply' or alternatively 'Pretty girl required'. Also use of words that suggest the sex of applicants . . er . . 'milkman', 'cleaning woman', 'waitress' as opposed to 'waiting person'. Words that suggest the sex of applicants are banned. There are a number of exceptions of course. Er . . that includes jobs that really can only be done by a man or a woman . . er . . um . . what . . a male warden in a men's hostel or housemother in a . . in a girls' school. Or for instance jobs that do require a resident couple. Another exception is in adverts for jobs in countries whose laws and customs are such 'that duties could not be performed effectively by a woman'.

Presenter: Well, advertisements aside, employers are already controlled by the law, aren't they?

Tessa: Women – or men: the law applies to discrimination against men in favour of women too, you know – women cannot be discriminated against by an employer. Now, this covers women already working as well as those women who are applying for jobs. For example, four people apply for the same job: three of them are interviewed and one gets the job; now the only one not interviewed is the only woman. If she's equally well-qualified as the others she can appeal to the Equal Opportunities Commission and the employer can be prosecuted.

Presenter: You mentioned before jobs that only a man, or only a woman, can do. Does this apply to heavy manual labour too?

Tessa: Er . . theoretically, yes. An employer who refuses to give a job to a woman 'because women aren't strong enough to do heavy lifting', for example, is breaking the law. But he is within his rights to say to an individual woman: 'You're not strong enough.'

Presenter: Or to a man: 'You're not strong enough' presumably?

Tessa: Yes, yes, certainly. These rules don't apply to all employers, by the way. A company with fewer than six employees is exempt. There are other so-called Protective Laws, which forbid employers from employing women for over 48 hours a week, or making them start before 7 a.m. In factories, in . . in manual jobs that is – not in management or clerical jobs. I'm not really sure if these laws are to protect women or to protect their husbands and children from neglect! However, no laws can protect working wives from the burden of having to do two jobs: one at the factory and another full-time one at home looking after her family.

(Time: 5 minutes 10 seconds)

3.8   Who tells the truth?   *Listening*

This is a scripted news report. Before they listen to the recording for the first time, students should try to *predict* who the missing categories of people are in the chart.

Answers

a) 85%   b) doctors   c) teachers
d) judges   e) 25%   f) 33%   g) person in the street   h) civil servants   i) 25%   j) 25%   k) 75%
l) trade union leaders   m) 71%   n) politicians generally
o) government ministers

Discussion ideas are given in the Student's Book.

Transcript

Correspondent: A public opinion poll published in today's *Times* reveals what people in the street think about who is to be trusted in the world today.

Top of the poll came clergymen – of

the people questioned 85% thought that they tell the truth. Next came doctors, closely followed by teachers and judges. Watching someone on television reading the news may inspire confidence in some viewers, but exactly one in four said they don't believe newsreaders. One in three said that they don't believe what members of the police force say, although 61% do seem to trust their 'friendly neighbourhood bobby'. Most doubt was expressed about a category of people it's impossible to pigeonhole accurately .. er .. presumably because anyone can fit into it, if they are in the right place at the right time! The 'person in the street' was however trusted by 57% of the people questioned.

Only one in four said that they believe what civil servants and business leaders say and journalists too were mistrusted by the people questioned with as many as three out of four saying they told lies. With business leaders disbelieved by so many, it's surprising then that their traditional opponents were even more under suspicion, with 71% of the people questioned saying that they were sure that trade union leaders don't tell the truth.

Finally, and not unexpectedly, came politicians with three out of four saying that they are just as much liars as the journalists are, and only 16% said that they thought that government ministers tell the truth. It might be interesting to know what the same members of the public think about public opinion polls and whether they tell the truth about what the public is thinking!

(Time: 2 minutes)

3.9 Twins

Picture conversation

Working in pairs, one partner looks at the photograph in activity 3, the other at the one in 42. The conversation is about relationships between brothers and sisters. If, by any chance, a member of the class *is* a twin, then he or she could be 'interviewed' by the whole class about the experience.

Encourage students to answer the questions at length, not just to say the simplest thing that comes into their head. Encourage questioners to pursue their line of questioning further if any other aspects of family life seem relevant to the conversation.

3.10 Past and Present

Communication activity

Working in groups of three, one student looks at 'Past and Present, No 1' by Augustus Egg (1858) in activity 73, another at 'Past and Present, No 2' in activity 6 and the third at 'Past and Present, No 3' in activity 79.

These three Victorian narrative paintings form three tableaux from the same melodramatic story. They illustrate the fate of an unfaithful wife (is the husband reading the lover's letter?) who tells her mother of her shame (does she condemn or sympathise with her daughter?) and, now a 'fallen woman', is about to drown herself in the Thames (will she have second thoughts?). There should, however, be enough ambiguity here for many different versions to be produced within the class. To tell the story students will have to work out together what happened before and after each of the scenes.

Ask the groups to narrate their versions of the story to the rest of the class. How differently would the same story have turned out in, for example, a present-day soap opera?

3.11   Description of a person   *Composition*

Discussion of the sample composition should take place in groups or pairs. Perhaps ask different groups to rewrite different parts of it and then report their improvements to the rest of the class.

Point out that one of the important things to control when writing a composition is REGISTER – suiting the style of the writing to the kind of situation and reader for which it is intended. The sample would be perfectly appropriate in an informal monologue or speech, or perhaps in a letter to an intimate friend. Take a look at some of the passages in this book: how would you characterise the register or style of them? What particular features seem typical of a particular register? (2.3 and 3.3 might be good places to start.) How can one become aware of the features of different registers – by reading widely and by stopping to analyse the style occasionally? Or can it just be absorbed while reading different kinds of texts?

Refer back to section E of 3.1 before students write their compositions. Pay particular attention to register and style when marking them.

4 Other places

4.1 Vocabulary

To start students off by thinking about different places in the world, you could do section D first. Make sure everyone can say and spell the countries correctly in English. The exercise should be done in pairs. If section A seems too difficult for them, it can be read through by you with all the necessary gaps filled – then they can fill in the gaps as they remember the missing words.

Answers

A 1 port   2 bay   3 harbour   4 plain   5 range of hills
6 lagoon   7 sandbank (*or* reef)   8 marshes (*or in tropical zones* swamps)   9 headland   10 cliffs   11 mouth   12 estuary
13 tributaries *or* streams   14 source   15 coastline   16 low tide   17 high tide   18 currents   19 scenery   20 view

B 21 holidaymakers, pilgrims, travellers   22 courteous, easygoing, hospitable   23 off the beaten track, out of the way, secluded
24 broadens the mind, gives you new experiences, widens your horizons
25 away from home, in foreign parts, out of the country
(Make sure time is spent considering the meanings of the *wrong* answers too.)

Section C may seem deceptively easy – but many advanced students still have difficulty in using English place names and nationality words, particularly when they are very similar in their own language. In a monolingual class, this section can be done as a class with one student standing at the board drawing frontiers and adding names of countries as the others give instructions.

Discussion ideas

Get students to describe the area in which they are studying, contrasting it with another area they know well (where relations live, where they go for holidays, or where they live when they're not studying).
Section D in the Student's Book is another discussion idea.

4.2 Learning the language

<u>Background</u>   Rose Macaulay's best-known novel, *The Towers of Trebizond* (1956), is an amusing account of travels made with an eccentric aunt in Turkey – a work of fiction, based presumably on real experiences. The passage here is, one assumes, factual, though if you know Turkish you may have doubts about this!

Students should discuss their answers in pairs.

Answers

1 By saying things loudly and repeatedly.
2 Both were very confused, but as the Turks gave up after a time, probably the author's confusion lasted longer.
3 Because there *was* a Mr Yorum in the hotel.
4 She had learnt the wrong phrase.
5 After.
6 He thought she wanted to speak to him.
7 She thought he was offering his services as interpreter.
8 None whatsoever.
9 Because there is always so much confusion in Turkey that she didn't think it mattered.
10 Judging from the passage it's just the name of a person.

Continuation:
Several more times on other days I told them I didn't understand Turkish, and each time they rang Mr Yorum and he came, and sometimes I paid for the drinks and sometimes he did. He and the hotel staff must have thought I had taken a great fancy to him or else that I was working up to some deal I wanted to do with him. The fourth time he came I had a bright idea that I would give him one of the Mowbray manuals that aunt Dot had left behind in her haversack, because I thought she would wish me to continue her Anglican work on the natives, and also each manual which I got rid of would lighten the haversack. So I went and got this manual, which was called 'Why I belong to the Church of England,' and was slightly translated into Turkish, and I gave it to Mr Yorum, who thanked me and looked at it with surprise, and it must have dawned on him that I was a missionary and was trying to convert him and that this was why I kept sending for him.

  After that he must have told the hotel staff not to ring him for me again, for when I said please to telephone him at once they shrugged and threw out their hands and looked at me despisingly.

Discussion ideas What does everyone think happened next in the
story? Have you had any similar embarrassing or
amusing experiences with English or another foreign language? Do you find
phrase books useful? What did you find amusing about the passage? Why
did it amuse you? Or leave you cold?

4.3   The sand baggers   *Reading*

A   shovelled – dug   overgrazing – eating too much vegetation
nomads – people with no fixed homes   precarious – insecure
funded – paid for   super dune – abnormally large dune   barbed
wire – wire with sharp spikes

B   1   Animals eating too much; not enough care; alteration in climate
    2   Main road getting blocked; semi-permanent homes; no agricultural
        produce
    3   Building cities (??); erecting wooden fences; seedlings with long stems;
        seedlings that will eventually grow long roots; abnormally large dune
    4   They allow animals to eat any plants; they must learn
    5   Secret and mysterious

C   Fibre glass panels: humorous with hint of serious intent
    Difficulties of the people: unsympathetic or perhaps wry humour
    Efforts of scientists: admiration

Discussion ideas Can you find examples to justify your answers to
the questions in section C? What is your opinion
about the fibre glass art idea? What would it be like to be a Mauritanian? Or
a dune project scientist?

4.4   Positive and negative   *Use of English*
sentences

Answers

2   The weather always seems better abroad than it does at home, doesn't
    it?
3   It's unpleasant to be alone in a strange country, isn't it?
4   Hardly any of the people/anyone in Britain speak(s) my language.
5   Not everyone in the world can be expected to understand your own
    language, can they?
6   Nothing you say would persuade me to live overseas.

7   There's nothing I wouldn't do to be able to travel to China.
8   There's nobody in Japan who doesn't speak Japanese.
9   I'm seldom able to afford to spend my holidays abroad.
10   Nowhere is as nice as your own country, is it?

4.5 Comparative and superlative sentences   *Use of English*

Some students may need hints to fill the gaps appropriately. For instance: 'not many people in Australia' or 'a long way west, Portugal'.

Answers

2 colder than   3 more mountainous than
4 polluted as the   5 trees/forests than
6 densely populated country than the   7 most westerly country in
8 as much rainfall as in   9 most powerful nations in the
10 coldest/most inhospitable continent in the

4.6 The vanishing island and dog soup   *Questions and summary*

Both articles appeared in *The Guardian* in 1984.

    Students should <u>underline</u> the words for explanation in the places they occur in the passages. In questions 3 and 5 discuss how the ideas can be paraphrased in different words.

Answers

1 superstition – belief   reluctant – unwilling   lush – rich
   conceivable – possible
2 it (line 17) – the island   It (line 19) – the disappearance   it (line 33)
   – the disappearance   This (line 39) – the local superstition
   This (line 50) – the destruction of vegetation and trees
3 fishermen may have dynamited the surrounding reefs; the vegetation and
   trees were probably cut down by local people leaving the island
   vulnerable to the monsoon winds and high seas which might have washed
   it away; tourists collecting shells may have opened up a hole in the coral –
   the island may then have poured away into the sea
4 image – reputation in the eyes of the world   ban – prohibition
   phased out – closed in stages   suit – be agreeable/acceptable to
5 to improve country's image for 1986 Asian Games and 1988 Olympics;
   protests from US and European dog-lover organisations; foreign tourists
   have been offended by the sight of dog carcasses

4.7 Three island nations   *Listening*

Give students time to anticipate the answers to the questions by looking at them together before they hear the recording.
The recording is part of a radio interview. It may help some students to be shown the whereabouts of the three countries on a globe or map of the world.

Answers

SINGAPORE   Chinese, Malay, Tamil   hot and humid   flat
2½ million   food and customs   beaches   hot

NEW ZEALAND   270,000 sq km   cool   warm   3,000 m
½ million   spectacular   cold, damp and miserable

PAPUA NEW GUINEA   3 million   Pidgin and 750 local languages
hot and humid   4,000 m   40,000
unspoilt   wet

Transcript

Interviewer: Three places that have been much in the news this week feature in a new travel brochure, offering holidays only on islands. They are Singapore, New Zealand and Papua New Guinea. Dr Alan Roberts of Exeter University has visited all three countries and is Reader in Asian and Pacific Studies. Alan, how much do these places have in common?

Alan: Well, in terms of size, very little. Er . . Singapore for example is tiny . . um . . smaller than, say, New York City. But . . er . . New Zealand is larger than the United Kingdom, that's got a total area of 270,000 square kilometres. Now, Papua New Guinea, that's . . er . . mm . . twice the size . . er . . larger than California, say. As regards population, now they . . they are similar, they're all around 3 million. Now when you come to talk about languages there's a considerable difference there. There's four official

languages in Singapore: that's Chinese, Malay, Tamil and English. But . . er . . Papua New Guinea has an amazing 750 local languages, many of which are . . .

Interviewer: Oh, I say!

Alan: Yes, I know, yeah. Many of which are unique and completely unrelated to any other language . . um . . but the main language of the . . er . . island is Pidgin. Um . . weatherwise both Singapore and Papua New Guinea are tropical with . . um . . hot, humid weather all year, but New Zealand, well that's similar to Western Europe with cool winters and warm summers. Um . . of course, their winter's when our summer is and vice versa. Um . . both New Zealand and Papua New Guinea are . . are very mountainous. Many peaks of the South Island of New Zealand, for example, are . . um . . over 3,000 metres, and in the thickly forested Central Highlands of the . . Papua

New Guinea, well, could be over 4,000 metres. Singapore, however; flat, complete contrast.

Interviewer: And er . . how about tourism? Um . . I understand a major part of the economy of each country depends on visitors from overseas.

Alan: Yes. Yes. Well, that m . . particularly true of Singapore: er . . 2½ million visitors every year, they get. New Zealand: still . . well . . pretty undeveloped . . er . . perhaps not surprisingly . . er . . bearing in mind that it's quite a long way away for people to get to, it's . . er . . only half a million visitors there. And Papua New Guinea: still developing its tourist industry . . er . . running at about 40,000 a year.

Interviewer: Mmhm. and . . um . . what would you say were the main attractions of each of these islands?

Alan: Yes, well, there's . . er . . plenty to see and do in . . in New Zealand if . . if you like the outdoor life. Er . . the scenery is spectacular. Um . . Singapore doesn't have those spectacular scenes . . er . . mountains and things but it has plenty of bargains for shoppers. Um . . its greatest attraction for me is perhaps its wide variety of different ethnic foods and customs . .

(Time 4 minutes 10 seconds)

um . . it's Asia in miniature, if you like. Er . . Papua New Guinea, on the other hand, is . . is largely s . . unspoilt still – it's . . er . . wild and relatively primitive and not very many . . er . . good roads, pretty accessi . . inaccessible in the interior. Um . . the only problem about Singapore, I suppose, is that it . . er . . it doesn't have any beaches but . . er . . it . . that's compensated by the fact that there are lots of hotels and they have swimming pools. Um . . I suppose if one's going to look for a problem with New Zealand is that it is pretty difficult to get to, it's inaccessible for many people and pretty costly to reach from . . um . . obviously lots of different parts of the world.

Interviewer: Yes. And . . er . . well, how about the weather? Does that present any problems for the visitor?

Alan: Well, I suppose that depends from where . . wh . . wh . . where you're coming from . . um . . Singapore can be very very hot if you're not used to that sort of weather . . um . . Papua New Guinea can be very very wet . . um . . and winter in New Zealand, if that's the time you're going, can be very cold, damp and pretty miserable.

Discussion ideas   What is the attraction of islands as holiday resorts? Describe an island that you know. Which of the three places described sounds most attractive to you and why? What are the features that you look for in your 'ideal' holiday place?

4.8   The impact of tourism   *Listening*

Students should read the questions before they hear the recording for the first time. The recording is a radio interview. The questions are relatively easy, so that students can listen to the recording 'for pleasure and interest' – the ideas expressed may provoke some interesting discussion, see below. (The information is based on material in *Diamonds in the Sky* by Kenneth Hudson and Julian Pettifer.)

Answers

True: 2, 3, 4, 5, 8, 10, 11
False: 1, 6, 7, 9, 12

Transcript

Presenter: Fiji is a group of tropical islands in the Pacific Ocean. Bill White has just revisited Fiji, where he worked during the early 70s. And he's been noticing how the island and islanders have changed. Bill, is Fiji the tropical holiday paradise that the holiday brochures tell us about?

Bill: Well, in many ways it still is – if you can get away from the main island and the capital Suva. Don't forget there are after all over 800 islands in the group, of which only one hundred are inhabited. One of the troubles is there's always been tension between the Indians, who comprise 50% of the population, and the Fijians, who surprisingly make up only 42%. The Indians tend to run the commercial life of the island, they have the businesses and the shops, whereas the Fijians own the land and are farmers and fishermen. The impact of tourism has now become very noticeable, though it is quite a late development. It only started in the late 60s. Um . . this came about because flights between America and Australia had to stop there to refuel. And visitors began to stop over in Fiji, to sample which was then . . er . . an unspoilt 'tropical paradise'. The tourists . . er . . now mainly tend to come from Australia and New Zealand, amounting to about 200,000 each year. And tourism is the major dollar earner of the islands now. However, for every dollar earned, 75 cents of that goes straight out of the country again to pay for what the tourists consume. You see, the visitors tend not to eat the local Fijian produce. They eat New Zealand meat and salads, drink Australian beer and orange juice, and the local farmers have been, well, just unable to cope with the international demands of the visitors. Fiji is a very fertile island but . . er . . agriculture, for some reason, has not been able to adapt. And it's cheaper to import food by air. There have been some bad effects of tourism on the people. Ah . . for example, the children tend to play truant from school to act as guides for the shoppers – that is local shopkeepers will pay them to grab tourists and pull them into *their* souvenir shops. Haha . . ironically . . many of the souvenirs they buy are not made locally at all, but are imported from places like Singapore and Hong Kong. Fijians were known for their friendliness and hospitality. Er . . this is something I noticed particularly when I was there before, but now alas you're beginning to see a sullenness creep into their character. People seem to dislike the visitors and 'friendly Fiji', as advertised in the holiday brochures, is no longer so apparent. These advertisements have d . . have devalued it.

Presenter: I see, what a shame. They do say that travel broadens the mind, do you agree?

Bill: Well, I'm beginning to doubt it. You see the international ho . . hotel chains have made each hotel look very much like another. So, if you look at the visitors in those hotels, they are also starting to look alike. They tend to be made up mainly of elderly widows on a world tour. They talk about the same things in the same accents, they . . they share the same opinions, they eat the same food of course, they .. they drink the same drinks. And, to hark back to something I said earlier, they will find themselves buying the same Hong Kong-made souvenirs all over the world. They travel on the same planes like so many registered parcels. And what is sad is that they are totally unaware of the local people and their aspirations, of *their* problems and *their* tragedies. Er .. travel in fact is starting to inspire not mutual understanding as we all hoped but mutual contempt. The only difference for the tourist between being at home and being abroad is the weather and the fact that they now have people to serve them and do the washing-up afterwards.

(Time 4 minutes 50 seconds)

Presenter: How do you see the future for Fiji?

Bill: Well, despite what I've said, I'm optimistic. Nadi International Airport is no longer an essential refuelling stop. The new long-range jets can now cross the Pacific non-stop and so many airlines have already pulled out. Fiji, well, it can't revert to how it was in the past, that's too much to ask, you can't put the clock back. But the number of tourists may stabilise at an acceptable level .. um .. Australia and New Zealand is after all quite a small market. And the relationship between the natives and the visitors may mature – as it has in Spain – into a sensible, businesslike one.

Discussion ideas

What is meant by a 'sensible, businesslike relationship'? Has the speaker exaggerated the way that all tourists look and behave alike? How are foreign tourists treated in your country? How do they behave there? If what the speaker says is true, why do people bother to travel thousands of miles for better weather and better service than they can get at home? Should countries like Fiji discourage tourists – or segregate them in hotel zones – to protect the local people from them?

4.9 Beauty spots   *Pronunciation*

Students work in groups of three. Each has a description of one of the places illustrated in the Student's Book, the others have to match it to the picture. Student A: activity 4, student B: 45, student C: 71.

The places illustrated are in this order: Looe (activity 71), Lynton and Lynmouth (4), Fowey (45).

The descriptions in the communication activities are printed in two versions: one normal and the other with catenation marked and with the text divided into 'breath-sized chunks'. This should help students to read more fluently. Listen to, comment on and give advice on pronunciation.

Ask the class to identify the source of the passages. Are they from guidebooks, advertisements or brochures? Exactly what details of the style and content seem to betray their source? How would the texts be different if you were to describe each place on the back of a postcard? Judging from the descriptions, which seems the most attractive place?

4.10   Faraway places   *Communication activity*

Student A looks at activity 8, student B at 47 and student C at 76. In this
'jigsaw' exercise each student has different information about the pros and
cons of travelling to South East Asia, Sri Lanka and the South Pacific, taken
from Thomas Cook's Rankin Kuhn *Far Away Places* brochure. (There
seems to be a trend for holiday brochures to be more frank about the places
they describe than they used to be.)

Encourage them to paraphrase the information they have, not just to read
bits of it aloud.

4.11   Description of a place   *Composition*

Without a fair amount of discussion, this exercise will not work well. If it
seems too time-consuming, section 2 can be done in class with different
groups concentrating on different aspects of the task. Best of all, get
students to discuss in class and then to write *two* compositions for
homework this time – just this once!

Point out the need for careful SELECTION AND ORDERING of the information.
Which points seem most relevant/important? Which are much less
important? Should all the pros be in one part and all the cons in another
part of the composition? If so, which should come first and what is the effect
of this?

What is the best method for MAKING NOTES: numbers to show sequence or
arrows or different colours? Let students explain their own techniques. Ask
students to submit their notes as well as their completed compositions for
each other and you to see.

5 The arts

(Listening exercise 5.8 might be done first of all.)

5.1 Vocabulary

Perhaps begin by discussing what the class understands by the term 'art'. Does it include popular music, cinema and television? Is 'art' something for the educated élite, or can it appeal to every class of society? Is an artist someone who is highly respected (and rewarded) in their country? What would life be like for the members of the class if there were no paintings to see, or no music to listen to, for example?

Be prepared to accept all plausible answers as correct in section A.

Answers

A 1 rock/jazz/pop   2 flute/accordion/bouzouki, *etc.*
3 performance/singing/music/interval   4 rehearsing   5 cast
6 audition   7 auction (sale)   8 fresco/icon/masterpiece, *etc.*
9 self-portrait/portrait, *etc.*   10 director, screenplay writer/script-writer, producer, cameraman, *etc.*   11 violin, cello, double bass, viola, *etc.*   12 trumpet, bassoon, clarinet, oboe, French horn, tuba, flute, saxophone, *etc.*   13 piano, harpsichord, organ, synthesiser, pianola, *etc.*

B *The answers are a matter of opinion and feeling. However, there are certain adjectives that are not normally qualified with* very, *as they are already superlatives. So, nos. 15, 17 and 19 cannot have these adjectives used in them:*
superb, brilliant, great

C 21 dramas, plays, tragedies   22 play by ear, read music, read a score
23 reviews, trailer, write-ups   24 quintet, trio, quartet   25 band, group, orchestra

Discussion ideas

(See above.) What is the difference between 'art' and 'show business'? Is there such a thing as 'low-brow' art, or is this just 'entertainment'? Do you have to be knowledgeable about an art form to appreciate it?

5.2 Silent movies

Reading

<u>Background</u>   The passage comes from the introduction to a
history of the silent movie, published to
accompany a TV series in 1979. The writer is an expert on the genre, who
has arranged the re-showing of many silent classics in their original versions
with live orchestral accompaniment. Silent movies died with the advent of
the first talkie in 1926, 'The Jazz Singer'.

Answers

1   Magic: power to draw audiences into story, use of imagination
2   Charm, other-worldliness, nostalgia
3   Rival entertainments (TV, radio, etc.) more accessible
4   Disapproving, sceptical
5   To escape from a harsh reality
6   Reality
7   Word of mouth
8   Palace and cathedral
9   Reading (fan magazines), clothes, furniture
10 All classes, rich and poor
11 Language barrier
12 A movie-goer in the heyday of the silent movie. To make the reader feel
    as if he or she shares this enthusiasm.

Discussion ideas are included in the Student's Book.

5.3 Sponsorship lives!

Reading

<u>Background</u>   Many areas of the arts in Britain, including
symphony orchestras and theatres, receive grants
from the government-funded Arts Council. As the sales of tickets are still
often insufficient to support arts events, many of them rely on commercial
sponsorship.

Answers

1   cutting expenses to the bone – reducing expenses to the minimum
    good will – popularity   dying on its feet – becoming much less
    common   push – persuade people to buy (the term is also used for
    drug dealing)   feeling an even colder wind – in much greater financial
    difficulties

2 about £17 million   3 about £46 million   4 with profits falling
they have less money available to spend   5 they are unpopular with
the public   6 because they are property developers – pulling down old
buildings and building new ones   7 smaller audience but longer-term
impact   8 attracts student customers   9 tobacco companies
turned to sports sponsorship   10 no more sporting events left to
sponsor   11 not such a long-term commitment now (3 years instead
of 6 or 7)   12 he's not disturbed by this and thinks they should be
grateful for what they get

<hr>

Discussion ideas   How are the arts supported in your country? Do
tobacco companies play a similar role in your
country – or are the kinds of advertisements that are banned in Britain
allowed? Which sports competitions (and teams) are sponsored in your
country? Should orchestras, theatres and arts festivals be self-supporting? Is
it just the privileged middle classes who benefit from subsidised arts? Which
of the arts do you find least appealing and why?

5.4 Linking words   *Use of English*

Background   The passage is part of the preface to *Visions
Before Midnight*, a collection of witty television
reviews. Clive James, an Australian, was formerly TV critic of *The
Observer*. Two more collections of his articles have been published and the
first volume of his autobiography *Unreliable Memoirs* was a best-seller.

(*The Glittering Prizes*, mentioned in the passage, was a very popular
'quality' drama serial by Frederick Raphael about a group of Cambridge
undergraduates and their lives and relationships after university.)

This is quite a challenging exercise. If you think your class can't face such a
challenge at this stage, read the whole text aloud to them with the gaps filled
before they do the exercise together. On the other hand, the challenge may
do them good! Be prepared to accept plausible alternatives to the answers
given below.

Answers   1 but   2 that   3 however   4 after all
5 even   6 incidentally   7 unless
8 and   9 while   10 when   11 What   12 but   13 When
14 because   15 But   16 while   17 since   18 in order to
19 for example   20 although

Discussion ideas   Do you share the writer's feelings about TV and
dinner parties and intelligent conversation? Would
you like to be paid to do one of the things you enjoy most, like watching TV

or going to the movies? What is the role of the critic? Does a TV critic (who records his reaction to an ephemeral programme) have a special kind of role? Do you (like most TV viewers) watch soap operas? Which is your favourite? Which is the worst one? Do people in your country watch as much TV as the British and the Americans (about 30 hours per week)? How has TV led to a deterioration in our lives? Or to an enrichment of our lives?

5.5 Idioms with PUT

Use of English

Answers

2 We put him off giving up his job to become a painter.
3 The opening of his one-man show has been put off until he recovers from his illness.
4 The success of our local theatre has put our city on the map.
5 They put pressure on the Arts Council to subsidise the newly-formed orchestra.
6 Don't put words into my mouth: I never said I hated ballet!
7 I can't put my finger on what it was that I disliked about the performance.
8 The show's lack of success can be put down to the poor reviews it received in the press.
9 Put your previous failures behind you and think of what your next venture might be.
10 A plan has been put forward to prevent valuable paintings being sold to collectors and galleries abroad.
11 Lack of government support has put paid to the plan to build the new museum in the city.
12 You really put your foot in it when you told him that he had no talent as a painter!

5.6 Guernica

Questions and summary

Background

The passage comes from the book that accompanied an amazingly lucid and stimulating TV series (in eight parts on BBC2) on 20th century painting, sculpture and architecture. The author is arts critic of the international news magazine *Time* and an Australian.

A larger reproduction of Guernica, if you can find one, will help the class to appreciate the passage more. The original is nearly 8 metres wide and is in the Prado Museum, Madrid.

A invective – verbal attack   archaic – belong to the past   bereaved –
whose husband, child or relative has recently died   paraphernalia–
pieces of equipment   ephemeral – living for a day, impermanent

B 1 by getting people to discuss the images in their works
  2 from mass media, especially television
  3 war photography
  4 as investment
  5 as wallpaper for the walls of the powerful; harmless

C Before 1937: artists thought they could influence political thought – even
change the world.
After World War II: photography replaced painting (eg concentration
camps).
Today: art as an investment for the rich, wallpaper for the powerful –
no political role.

Discussion ideas   Do you agree with the writer's views? What
influence could a painting (or other work of art)
have on your personal feelings or relationships? Does a critic perform a
useful function in explaining works of art as well as evaluating them?

5.7 Terms of Endearment   *Listening*

Parts A and B should be done during the first and second listenings to the
recording, respectively. The recording is part of a radio broadcast discussing
the latest video releases.

Answers

A James L. Brooks – director and writer of the screenplay; Jeff Daniels –
Flap Horton; John Lithgow – Emma's lover; Shirley MacLaine – Aurora
Greenway; Larry McMurtry – writer of the orginal novel; Jack
Nicholson – Garrett Breedlove; Debra Winger – Emma

B True: 1, 3, 6, 7, 8, 9, 12
  False: 2, 4, 5, 10, 11

Transcript

Presenter: So, Alison, what's new in
video this month?

Alison: Well, the best of a bunch of
films I would say is 'Terms of Endear-

ment'. This is a film directed by James L. Brooks, who also wrote the screenplay. It's based on a novel by Larry McMurtry and it stars, as everyone knows, Shirley MacLaine and Jack Nicholson . . .

Presenter: Who both won Oscars, I think?

Alison: Yes, you're right they both did. Um . . now, I'm personally a great fan of Shirley MacLaine and she plays a character, a widow called Aurora Greenway, who lives in Houston, Texas, and is at the start of the film trying to persuade her daughter Emma, who's played by an excellent young actress called Debra Winger, whom I've not seen before but I thought was perfectly splendid . . er . . trying to persuade her not to marry Flap Horton, who's played by Jeff Daniels, who's also a newcomer to me. However, fairly early on in the film they do marry in spite of their mother and she continues, however, to have a . . a . . . . a terrific influence on her daughter's life and to rule it. But the daughter tries very hard to be free and the whole situation is not helped by the fact that . . er . . Aurora the mother dislikes her new son-in-law quite intensely.

Presenter: I think she boycotts the wedding in fact, is that right?

Alison: Yes, I bel . . yes, you're quite right there too, and she's given to very barbed remarks . . um . . to . . to both of them to try and . . er . . get in their way, such as . . er . . 'You aren't special enough to overcome a bad marriage' she says to her daughter. Er . . then as time passes, the son-in-law gets a teaching post at a university in Iowa, which is 1,000 miles away, to which mother says sarcastically: 'You can't even fail locally'. Um . . they

have more children than they can afford. Flap starts having affairs with his students . . um . . which Emma doesn't realise, Emma the daughter doesn't realise until she actually sees him with another girl one day. So to get her own back she begins a sad affair with a local banker, who's played by John Lithgow – a very nicely understated performance, I thought. Meanwhile Aurora herself is having an affair with her neighbour – he's lived next door for 15 years and this is a character who's a former astronaut, Garrett Breedlove, who's a . . now become a hard drinker . . played . . . Yes . . . And he's played by Jack Nicholson, who I must say does play this kind of character absolutely excellently. Yes. And . . and . . this is a terrific performance, terrific. Um . . they're very happy together in this relationship but he won't commit himself to a permanent relationship, so Aurora becomes very unsure of herself. Finally, towards the end of the film, Emma gets cancer and dies in hospital tragically, saying goodbye to her children and her husband.

Presenter: A 'Love Story'-type ending.

Alison: Yes, it is. I mean you could just say that it is just basically high-class soap opera, but the performances are great. There are some very good one-liners, especially from the . . er . . Jack Nicholson and Shirley MacLaine characters. It's an Oscar-winning movie, after all. It does work, however, better on video than it did on the big screen, I'm convinced of that. I found it very enjoyable. It's got some serious ideas about relationships too, even . . even though it is just soap, and I recommend it very highly indeed.

Presenter: Thank you, Alison.

(Time: 3 minutes 30 seconds)

53

Discussion ideas Is an Oscar-winning performance or movie usually a great one? Think of some films you've seen that have been awarded Oscars. Do you enjoy films like the one described, or do you avoid them like the plague? What is the greatest film ever made, in your opinion? And which was the worst you've ever seen?

5.8 Starlight Express   *Listening*

Another radio discussion about more middle-brow (or low-brow?) entertainment. Andrew Lloyd Webber, who seems to have the Midas touch when it comes to musicals, also wrote the music for 'Evita' and 'Jesus Christ Superstar'. He seems to specialise in putting daft-sounding ideas on the stage and making them into hit musicals.

After reading the questions through beforehand, students should aim to get all the answers on just *one* listening.

Answers 1 silly 2 somewhat disappointing
3 different styles 4 Frances Ruffelle
5 'Only You' 6 the sound system was very loud 7 forgettable
8 incredible 9 scared 10 touching 11 excited
12 profundity 13 popular

Transcript

Paul: Celia Clarke of *The Daily Telegraph* and I have been to see Andrew Lloyd Webber's musical 'Starlight Express' at the Apollo Theatre. Celia . . um . . are you a fan of Andrew Lloyd Webber?

Celia: Not exactly, no. I did quite enjoy 'Evita', it did have its one good song 'Don't Cry for me, Argentina', but apart from that I thought the story was rather silly. I didn't like 'Cats', th . . that only had one good song 'Memory' and some very good dancing.

Paul: Oh, I . . I would have thought that 'Cats' had more than just the one good song, but . . er . . I thought, you know, I thought it was really very good, but . . er . . back to 'Starlight Express'.

Celia: Yes, well, 'Starlight Express'. Here all the characters are machines,

not animals, they're all machines. All the men play the locomotives, the engines, and all the women play the various carriages – on roller skates. It's quite amazing, there's a track across the stage, over the stalls and on a bridge that comes right across in front of the dress circle. It's a . . a millionaire's train set open to the public. And a lot of the seats were taken out of the theatre to make room for these amazing race tracks.

Paul: Yes, technically . . er . . quite amazing. Um . . but what did you think of the story?

Celia: Haha. Well, er . . there's virtually none. I suppose it deals with the preparation for and the staging of a . . a race between trains from all over the world. Different locomotives and carriages sing their songs and the diesel and the electric engines, the new

54

flashy ones, are mostly unreliable and gradually knock each other out of the different race stages until at the final the good old honest steam train wins and gets the girl, but that's all there is to it!

Paul: Yes, but I . . I thought the songs were particularly good and . . and clever. I . . think he's a master of the pastiche . . er . . different styles: 50s, 70s, don't you?

Celia: Yes, yes, clever. Yes, clever. We had . . er . . Jeff Shankly as Greaser, as a rock 'n'roll character in . . in true Elvis Presley style. And wonderful Frances Ruffelle as Dinah the Dining Car, with her country and western song 'Uncoupled', particularly clever . . clever number that one. And Jeffrey David as the explosive character, the electric loco . . um . . aptly named Electra, and he has a David Bowie-style showstopper, called 'AC/DC'. The . . .

Paul: Yes. Yes. What did you think was the best song?

Celia: Well, er . . the . . *the* song of the show . . er . . like, for instance 'Memory' and 'Don't Cry for me, Argentina', the song of the show is Stephanie Lawrence's 'Only You', which has been released as a single. Er . . yes, all the songs were well performed.

Paul: I thought the lyrics were clever too . . um . . written by Richard Stilgoe.

Celia: Yes, of course, he is a brilliant lyric writer, exceedingly clever. Er . . unfortunately . . er . . particularly with the . . the song I mentioned earlier 'Uncoupled' it was difficult to hear them. The high volume . . er . . of the speakers all round the theatre was absolutely, absolutely deafening, which was a shame. One wants to sit down and listen to them all again to get the . . the lyrics. But I think the main point is that . . er . . all the tunes were fairly unmemorable. Can you . . can you hum any to me now?

Paul: Yes I . . no, I think I go along with

that. I think it's a . . it is a visual, it's an effects type of show. I thought . . I thought the choreography by Arlene Phillips and the staging by the director Trevor Nunn . . um . . particularly . . er . . fine. Um . . he of course responsible for the direction of 'Cats', so he's obviously moved out of the Royal Shakespeare and that sort of thing. And the design of the production by John Napier particularly outstanding.

Celia: Oh, mind-blowing. Yes. An amazing amount was spent on . . on the production. I believe something in the region of £2 million. Visually it was superb. The races themselves were absolutely tremendous: each engine with several girl carriages hanging on behind, zooming all around the theatre at up to 40 miles an hour. Amazing noise. Danger when the b . . bridges have to come down and join on to each other. You . . you think it's never going to work. Cheering, excitement, oh amazing! It does sound very childish but it was extremely good, that's . . .

Paul: That was, and quite frightening for the audience, I thought.

Celia: Oh yes!

Paul: You know, as I say, you know, visually and . . er . . in terms of atmosphere . . um . . you know really very good indeed. Um . . w . . er . . any particular performances you'd single out?

Celia: Er . . well, they're all good singers and extremely good skaters. Um . . Rocky 1, 2 and 3 are . . a . . amazing . . n . . number they had the . . the threesome together. Er . . not particularly a lot of acting required, although Ray Shell as . . as Rusty, the steam engine hero, did pluck at the heart-strings and you definitely wanted him to win.

Paul: I've got a bit of a soft spot for Stephanie Lawrence, I must say, I mean I thought she was particularly good. Um . . I must say *I* left the . . the . . theatre feeling exhilarated . . er . . a

.. a unique experience I think really.

Celia: Absolutely, it was indeed. But .. er .. I .. I don't know. I felt a bit depressed about it. I mean, so much money and talent wasted on such .. well, really an empty story. Completely ephemeral. It's better to go roller-skating oneself than to see others doing it for you. Haha.

Paul: Well, maybe. Um .. true, .. I .. I won't say it's a great profound story but I .. I thought as entertainment goes I thought it was remarkable and .. er .. I think it should run for years, like .. er .. like 'Cats' and 'Evita' have done.

Celia: Oh, inevitable.

(Time: 6 minutes)

Discussion ideas Does the review tempt you to get seats for the show? What is it that attracts you to/puts you off seeing a musical like that? What are the ingredients that seem to make a show a hit or a flop? Has anyone in the class seen an Andrew Lloyd Webber show – or a similar kind of show? What is your reaction to two apparently serious-minded critics spending their time reviewing this kind of show?

5.9   Two paintings   *Picture conversation*

Student A looks at activity 26, student B at 44. The picture in 26 is a reproduction of an Edwardian painting of a young couple in a café with an older waiter; the picture in 44 is a modern airbrush painting of a young woman in a chair beside the portrait of an older man with the shadow of an approaching third person in the doorway. The discussion involves describing the pictures and evaluating them. Students also have a chance to talk about other favourite paintings.

5.10   What do you enjoy?   *Communication activity*

Student A looks at activity 9, student B at 46. Each has a list of questions to ask the other to find out about their tastes and experiences in the arts. Before they start talking they should make notes on their answers to their own questions.

5.11   A day in the life   *Composition*

Begin by discussing the article. What are students' feelings about this kind of performance art? Let them get their feelings of ridicule (?), amazement and disbelief off their chests so that they can apply themselves to the imaginative process of continuing the accounts. Probably male students should continue Tehching Hsieh's story and female students Linda Montano's. Unimaginative students may need some help in putting themselves into the artists' shoes.

Point out that in marking this composition you'll be paying particular attention to CORRECT SPELLING. Everyone should check their completed compositions through for spelling before handing them in. Most spelling mistakes at this level are 'careless' or 'silly' and can easily be spotted when checking work through.

6 The news

(Listening exercise 6.7 might be done first of all.)

6.1 Vocabulary

Perhaps begin by giving a brief survey of the British press, if this seems
appealing, showing students some actual copies of different British or at
least English language newspapers if possible. How many students read a
paper every day? Most days? Very rarely?

Answers

A 1 editorial *or* leader (column)   2 tabloids   3 communiqué/
statement/press release   4 correspondent   5 spokesman/spokes-
person/minister (?)   6 earthquake/hurricane/typhoon, *etc.*
7 coverage   8 topical   9 misprint/mistake   10 section/page

B 11 More than   unemployed/out of work   12 reaction   coal
mines/pits   13 victims   earthquake   14 Conservative
election   15 attempt   reconcile   16 disappointment
17 Ambassador   flown   attend a debate   18 their jobs
19 Prime Minister   controversy/criticism   20 identity
organiser   21 Three   arrested/charged   22 received/accepted/
taken   resigned/been fired   23 Soviet   increased   24 seized
worth   25 Negotiations   fishery   held

Discussion ideas   (See above.) What do the members of the class
expect to find in a good newspaper? What is a
'good newspaper'? Does a paper have to express the same political views
that you hold to be acceptable to you? With TV news providing immediate
coverage of news soon after it has happened, what is the function of a daily
newspaper? Or of a weekly news magazine?

6.2 Three news reports *Reading*

The Times and *The Guardian* are 'quality' dailies, *The Daily Mail* is a not-too-sensational tabloid. The reports appeared on the same day in 1984.

You might be able to find similarly conflicting reports by looking through this week's newspapers and showing them to the class.

Answers	1) B and C	2) A	3) B	4) A and B
	5) C	6) B	7) A	8) A	9) B

10 C   11) A   12) B   13) C   14) B   15) A and C   16) B

Discussion ideas   Do discrepancies like these matter? Would there be similar mistakes in more weighty news reports? What can you believe in a news report – in a paper, or on the radio or TV? Why do we bother to read reports like these which obviously don't really affect us personally? Do such reports have a place in serious papers like *The Times*?

6.3 Three sports reports *Reading*

Tennis is one of the few sports played by both sexes all over the world. Nonetheless, many of your students will probably know little about it – this doesn't matter. As long as they know what Wimbledon is and are prepared to work out meanings of unfamiliar words from their contexts, they should be able to appreciate the reports and answer the questions.

Point out that to answer the questions, it is necessary to search for the information and to *disregard* irrelevant parts of the articles.

Answers

1 *Mail*: 5   *Guardian*: 1½
2 Nothing (except 'a pageant of rich language'??)
3 *The Guardian* ('You piss me off')
4 *Times*: 6   *Guardian*: ½   *Mail*: 1 (one sentence long!)
5 Simone Colombo's spitting at a linesman was worse
6 Arias did beat Ocleppo and Lendl did beat Tarr. The rest are false.
7 Imagery: 'unfurled his colours'; 'sow ... grunting in her sty'; 'off his feed'; 'unleashed'; 'barrage'; 'every inch of the canvas'; 'back on his feed', etc.
  Idioms: 'roll on to victory'; 'the heart of the matter'; 'seal the match'; 'meat and drink'; 'on his usual high plateau', etc.

Discussion ideas Which report gives the best impression of the match? Can a report in a paper describe a sporting event adequately? What is your reaction to the slant of the *Daily Mail* article – would a straight match report be preferable, or less interesting?

6.4 Past, present and future forms *Use of English*

Answers

2 Admission charges will no longer be made in museums.
3 A headmaster who caned a pupil has been cleared of criminal charges.
4 A man with a gun has killed three people in a bank robbery.
5 The police have solved the mystery of the heiress who disappeared.
6 The police have been attacked in a violent demonstration.
7 A student leader has claimed that the police attacked the demonstrators.
8 Parents and pupils are protesting about a head teacher's decision to send pupils with long hair home. (?)
9 The city council is going to control/ban striptease shows.
10 Customs officials have seized one million pounds' worth of smuggled goods/drugs.

6.5 Reporting speech *Use of English*

Answers
2 would be   3 that many   would be
4 that there was   5 that she would be withdrawing   6 that he was disappointed/satisfied/delighted, *etc.*
7 that there would be/could be   8 how they had been rescued
9 that   will be spent on   10 that the   would (not)

6.6 A correspondent's life *Questions and summary*

It was Michael Buerk's BBC TV reports on the famine in Ethiopia (see 12.3) which alerted the world to the situation there.

After the students have made notes in answer to question 8, direct them to communication activity 58, where there is a set of model notes to compare with theirs. Later, when they have written their paragraphs, they can look at activity 31, where a complete written paragraph is shown. How do their versions compare with the model?

1 shuffling on the landing – noise of moving feet outside the room
insouciance – not caring   itchy feet – wanting to travel   fronting –
being the presenter   dovetail – fit neatly
2 noise of men waiting in queues outside the rooms near his
3 plenty of wine and amusing reading matter to keep the men happy
4 looking for scorpion
5 paid to go all over world to see most interesting and important events
6 being recognised; treated as 'important'
7 12 times . . . effect of dramatic pause in speech; seems overdone in print
8 See communication activity 58 and, subsequently, 31.

Discussion ideas   Compare the model versions with students' own
versions. What would it be like to have Michael
Buerk's job? Do you envy him? Why (not)? What difference does it make to
see a TV on-the-spot report, rather than hear a newsreader give the same
information? Does a correspondent tend to give a biased version of events?

6.7 What do you read?   *Listening*

In the recording eight different people are interviewed. Perhaps an
exceptionally well-informed class might attempt to identify the papers and
magazines they described? They were (though this is not essential
information for students): Bill: *The Times* (its 'bingo' is called '*The Times
Portfolio*' and is based on the movements of stocks and shares – the game
boosted the circulation of the paper appreciably); Jerry: a foreign English
language paper; Ann: *Sunday Times* (or *Observer*); Ken: *The Guardian*;
Michael: *Newsweek* (or *Time*); Yvonne: a local evening paper; Ted (*The
Sun* – which has a girlie photo on page 3 – or *The Mirror* or *The Star*);
Harry: *The Guardian Weekly* (which is normally available only on
subscription, not in shops – highly recommended!)

Answers

Bill: Morning daily   UK
           Likes: news of Britain, world news, bingo
           Dislikes: editorials
Jerry: Morning daily (?)   Elsewhere
           Likes: news of USA, price
           Dislikes: quality of printing, political standpoint
Ann: Sunday   UK
           Likes: good writing, colour, arts (well, books, anyway)
           Dislikes: business

Ken: Morning daily   UK
      Likes: entertainment, good writing, arts, TV
      Dislikes: cartoons
Michael: Weekly   USA (?)
      Likes: news of Britain, USA, world, photographs
      Dislikes: advertisements
Yvonne: Evening daily   UK
      Likes: news of Britain (well, local news), advertisements
      Dislikes: advertisements (cars and houses)
Ted: Morning daily   UK
      Likes: entertainment, takes short time to read, photographs (on page 3)
      Dislikes: bingo
Harry: Weekly   UK
      Likes: entertainment, good writing, news of USA and world
      (*Washington Post* and *Le Monde*)
      Dislikes: nothing

Transcript

Presenter: We asked a number of people to tell us about their favourite newspaper or magazine and to say, first of all, why they bought it, then what page they looked at first, then what it was they disliked about it. The first person we talked to was Bill.

Bill: Er . . well, the reason why I choose this particular newspaper is it . . it has an excellent coverage of news . . er . . both domestic and foreign. Its reports are serious and . . er . . unbiased, I . . I think that's particularly important. It . . it's an influential paper . . ha . . well, like the advertisement says . . the 'top people's newspaper'. Er . . the first thing I . . I look at is the . . the bingo. I look to see if I've won a prize . . er . . I haven't been lucky yet, but the other day I was only just . . er . . two points away from it. Um . . it can be a bit stuffy . . um . . a bit boring some of the time, particularly the leaders . . er . . yes . . er . . wh . . what about you, Jerry?

Jerry: Er . . well . . er . . the only English language paper published where I live . . er . . is the one that I read . . er . . for obvious reasons. It keeps me up to date . . er . . with the current events in Europe . . er . . although . . er . . not very well, but the imported English and American papers are very expensive and . . er . . they're not always available and . . er . . so there's no point in having a newspaper unless it's easy to get. Er . . the first thing I look about is news about Canada . . er . . which is very rare or . . er . . news about the . . the States. Um . . well, what do I dislike about it? It's not very well written and . . er . . there are printing mistakes and . . er . . it's very, very conservative. Um . . and what about you, Ann?

Ann: Well, I get this particular paper because the articles are so interesting and the book reviews are really good . . er . . and I always look forward to those. Um . . there are many very well-known writers and critics who are quite influential and I always enjoy reading . . er . . their articles. It just makes my Sunday mornings bearable really. Um . . I usually turn to the colour magazine first thing. Um . . what don't I like about it? Well, I suppose the business section really,

I'm not particularly interested in that, the only part I do read is the back page which often has quite interesting reports about new inventions and discoveries. Ken, your turn.

Ken: Um . . well, I like it, it's . . um . . intelligent . . er . . irreverent, witty, damn good read, you know, all those things that they say newspapers should be. Um . . the first thing I look at is the arts pages, very, very good coverage of arts and that's every day of the week . . um . . not just when there's something particularly that's opened that needs to be reviewed . . um . . at weekends the TV programmes, there's a very good coverage of . . er . . comprehensive . . er . . coverage of TV programmes. Er . . what I don't like . . er . . are the strip cartoons, I don't understand them . . er . . and they're very crudely drawn. Er . . Michael, over to you.

Michael: Mm . . (*cough*) . . . Yes, well . . um . . the thing that I like about this magazine is it's got good readable reports from all over the world, it's a s . . you know, you read it once a week and you know what's going on, it's all over the world, not just . . er . . England and . . er . . the United States, So . . er . . it's very well researched and I . . I believe, you know, it's got integrity and I believe . . um . . what I read in it, I know what's going on. Um . . the first thing I do is I flip through and look at the photos, that way you can tell which articles will be of the most interest to you, and I go back and I read it all the way through and I . . er . . course I don't like the advertising, there's more and more advertising all the time and . . er . . ads for things like gold watches and first class air travel, which most people can't afford. But . . er . . it's a small price to pay really. Um . . what do you read, Yvonne?

Yvonne: Well . . er . . I . . er . . don't get much time to read the morning papers, so . . er . . I get this because it tells me what's happening locally and there are lots of adverts in it for local shops and . . and cinemas and that. Um . . I suppose I . . I look first at the . . er . . at the main headlines, at the main story, the main article, I suppose. Everybody does, don't they? Um . . the only problem with it, as far as I'm concerned, is that there are lots of adverts in it for things I . . I'm not particularly interested in, you know, like cars for sale and houses and that. Wh . . what about you, Ted?

Ted: Well, it's easy to read, it's pretty entertaining, it doesn't take too long to get through it. I mean, you could read it in your tea break really, you shove it in your back pocket, you know. Um . . the first thing I look at is page 3, but . . er . . don't tell the wife! Er . . what I don't like about it is the bingo, I mean everyone knows . . it . . it's fixed, I mean that's . . it's just a con and I know there's no chance of me winning. All the winners happen on a Friday, anyway, for some reason. Er . . yeah. Harry, you're the last one.

Harry: Yes, well, there's so many reasons why I . . I read this . . er . . paper . . um . . let me see, what I really like is the selection of the best articles of the week, they . . they're not stuffy, they're amusing, entertaining, and enlightening. It takes hours to get through because . . er . . well, most of it is worth reading – unlike . . er . . some papers I could . . er . . mention. Um . . the first thing I look at are . . are the . . the articles from the *Washington Post* and *Le Monde* i . . in English. Um . . well, I don't dislike anything about it really, sometimes it's delayed in the post, that's all.

(Time: 5 minutes 20 seconds)

Which of the publications sounds most attractive? Answer the questionnaire about the paper or magazine *you* read. Compare your answers with the others in a group.

6.8   Here is the news   *Listening*

The recording is a radio news broadcast. Allow students time to read the questions through before they hear the recording.

Answers

True: 1, 3, 5, 11, 12, 13, 15, 19
False: 2, 4, 6, 7, 8, 9, 10, 14, 16, 17, 18, 20

Transcript

Brian: . . . and it's just coming up to 8 o'clock and it's time for the news. The air traffic controllers' strike is already hitting holidaymakers. Storms during the night have caused widespread damage in the western half of the country. Many people are feared dead in a typhoon in Japan. There's to be a summit meeting next month. A surprise result for Britain in the Italian tennis championships. With the details here's Susan MacMillan.

Newsreader: The strike which began at midnight of air traffic controllers at Heathrow and Gatwick has caused the cancellation of scores of flights today. The Association of Air Traffic Controllers has called out its members in protest against the Civil Aviation Authority's plans to rearrange their shift working system. Non-union members are not affected and management and supervisory staff are working double shifts in an attempt to minimise the disruption. Here's Larry Harrison with the details from Heathrow Airport.

Harrison: The latest from here is that there will inevitably be further cancellations and delays today and the situation is likely to deteriorate during the course of the day. British Airways say that they hope to get more than half of their flights away but that there will inevitably be delays of anything from one to three hours in departures. Many incoming flights have already been diverted to Stansted, Hurn and Birmingham. Gatwick is less badly hit, with incoming flights as yet unaffected and about 80% of outgoing flights subject to delays of no more than two hours. Calls have been made for the Advisory Conciliation and Arbitration Service (ACAS) to be called in but the unions are unwilling to agree to this at this time. Talks between management and unions which broke down on Friday have not been resumed.

Newsreader: The number to ring for flight information is 01 759 2525 for flights from Heathrow and information is also available on BBC Ceefax page 140.

   Storms yesterday in the West Country caused extensive damage and flooding. A report from Jenny Dawson of Radio Devon.

Dawson: After the worst storms this year, damage running into millions of pounds is reported to buildings throughout the South-West. Fourteen people were taken to hospital at Barnstaple after the coach they were travelling in was hit by a falling tree. None of them are said to be seriously hurt. A family of six had a lucky escape when their house caught fire after being struck by lightning in Appledore – they had left home only minutes before for their first visit to the cinema in five years. Elsewhere flooding has cut several major roads in Somerset, Devon and Dorset. The M5 motorway was closed for several hours last night near Wellington and the A30 and A303 have just been reopened now that floodwaters have receded. Other main roads are still affected and motorists are advised not to travel unless their journeys are essential and to check locally on road conditions.

Newsreader: Overseas the weather has been causing problems too. The southern Japanese island of Kyushu has been hit by the worst typhoon for many years and at least 20 people were killed when a landslide carried a train into a river near Kumamoto. The typhoon, which is showing no signs of blowing itself out, is nearing the heavily populated area of Kobe and Osaka. Train services on the famous high-speed Bullet train line from Tokyo to Hakata have been suspended for the first time since 1980.

Plans were announced late last night for an economic summit meeting to be held in Athens next month between the leaders of the United States, Britain, France, West Germany, Italy, Canada and Japan. A report from our economics editor Jonathan Greenlees.

Greenlees: The announcement of a summit meeting next month comes as a complete surprise, as does the choice of venue. No announcement has been made about the agenda for the meeting, but it's believed that it takes place at the request of France and Italy whose currencies have been under heavy attack from the dollar recently. Meetings of this kind are normally planned several months ahead and an emergency meeting would generally only take place in times of crisis. The place of these meetings would normally be in one of the seven countries concerned and it is rare for a 'neutral' city to be chosen. The only explanation seems to be that the leaders of Canada, Germany and Britain are all due to be holidaying in the Eastern Mediterranean next month.

Newsreader: News is just coming in of a possible settlement in the air traffic controllers' dispute. Controllers at Heathrow have agreed to allow their case to be taken to arbitration and have called off their action from midnight tonight. Gatwick controllers have yet to announce their decision. Flights in and out of Heathrow are still likely to be affected today and will not start to return to normal until tomorrow, when delays are still likely to occur.

Now sport. The British player John Lloyd has knocked John MacEnroe out of the Italian tennis championships in Rome. Our sports correspondent Bill Hardy.

Hardy: John Lloyd was on terrific form here in Rome. After losing the first set 4—6, he went on to beat MacEnroe 6—0, 7—6, 6—4. MacEnroe who pulled a muscle during the Wimbledon finals appeared to be unfit and troubled by his shoulder. He contested many of the line-judges' calls and received an official warning from the referee. After the first set, his service became weak and he appeared to be depressed and in pain. Lloyd, who is unseeded, goes on to meet Ivan Lendl in the next round. Lendl beat Vitas Gerulaitis in the third round and Lloyd is unlikely to do so well against him on this hard court.

Newsreader: Finally the weather. Western areas after last night's heavy rain

65

should be mainly dry today with scattered showers towards evening. Central and eastern parts will have heavy rain at first with some thunderstorms, but later in the day brighter weather may be expected. In the North and in Northern Ireland and Scotland temperatures will remain be- low normal but some sunshine can be expected. The outlook for tomorrow and the weekend: continuing unsettled in all areas tomorrow but with clearer weather spreading across from the west on Saturday. That's all from me in the newsroom, now back to Brian.

(Time: 6 minutes 15 seconds)

6.9   Animal stories   *Pronunciation*

Student A looks at activity 10 (about rats in China), B at 48 (about a rare bird) and C at 77 (about an eagle and a hang-glider). Each text is printed both in its original format and in an easy-to-read version.

After commenting on pronunciation, encourage them to remember or bring to class similar short news items they've seen in recent newspapers. Do they think such items are amusing, informative or just daft?

6.10   Sweet revenge   *Communication activity*

Student A looks at activity 11, student B at 50. In this 'jigsaw', A has parts one and three of the article, B has part two. They should use their own words to tell their partner about each part. Perhaps spend a little time as a class trying to guess what the article will contain, before students separate into pairs and look at the activities.

6.11   Two narratives   *Composition*

The notes and sequencing of events from the two articles should be discussed before students write their *two* compositions. If each one is about 100 to 150 words long, this should not take too long.

Point out that in marking the completed compositions you'll be paying particular attention to PUNCTUATION. When does one use a comma, or a dash, or a semi-colon or a full stop, for example? The 'rules', such as they are, in English are quite flexible. Take a look at some passages that have already been studied in this book to see how punctuation is used. Sentence length is also involved here. Long sentences may be transformed into shorter ones by using different punctuation – and vice versa.

7 Consumers

(Perhaps begin with listening exercise 7.7.)

7.1 Vocabulary

Perhaps start by asking students to think of as many different kinds of shops and eating places as they can in two minutes. What is most important for them when deciding where to shop: convenience, service, quality, price, choice, parking, friendly advice? Does it depend on what they want to buy: food, clothes, books, etc.?

Answers
1 consumers   2 discount/markdown
3 turnover/profit   4 brand   5 auction
6 bargain/haggle   7 shoplifting   8 hardware   9 fishmonger's *or* fishmongers   10 stationer's   11 delicatessen   12 take-away (shop)/fish and chip shop   13 hygiene   14 contravenes/breaks/flouts   15 deposit
16 arcade, shopping precinct, shopping centre   17 value for money, good value, a bargain   18 retailer, trader, vendor   19 manufacturer, supplier, wholesaler   20 customer, client, purchaser   21 transaction, sale, purchase made   22 delicious, tasty, wholesome
23 cider, soft drink, lager   24 on posters, in commercials, in press releases   25 courteous, helpful, good-natured

Discussion ideas   (See above.) How have shops and stores changed over the past 10 or 20 years? What kinds of shops have been closing down or going out of business? What kinds of shops have been opening up? Think of the area you live in. Where's the best place locally to get: fruit, bread and cakes, magazines, stationery, books, a snack, a good inexpensive meal, a good cup of coffee, smart inexpensive clothes for men and for women, tapes and records, etc.?

7.2 Tide turns against the Devil *Reading*

No previous knowledge is assumed in the article, but the jokey style may alarm some students. Perhaps begin by explaining the pun in the headline.

Answers

1 hirsute – hairy   tithe – payment of a tenth part   bedevil – cause trouble for
2 Satan, Lucifer, Old Nick, the Antichrist, Mephistopheles
3 'Satanic soap suds'; 'Lucifer in the loo'; 'satanic smear'; 'Antichrist allegations'; 'dividend for The Devil'; 'Mephistopheles in the market place'
4 moon: a popular image 131 years ago
  13 stars: original American colonies
5 Christians being urged to boycott P & G products
6 Disclaimers sent to 48,000 churches
7 Defamation suits against rumour-mongers
8 Yes – large ads denying story
9 Apparently not
10 Yes – part of 'urban folklore'

The tone: humorous/jokey/flippant. Use of word-play: 'cleanse the Devil', 'bedevil companies', 'satanic smear', etc.

Discussion

Perhaps introduce an example of another tale that belongs to urban folklore – stories that happened to a friend of a friend, like the one about the grandmother who died during a motoring holiday abroad: the body was put on the roof of the car and the car was stolen and the body and the car were never found again. Or the one about dead cats/rats/dogs being kept in the deep freeze of a Chinese/Indian restaurant. What similar stories do members of the class have to tell?

7.3 How we test fridges *Reading*

Which? is a consumer magazine, available only to members of the Consumers' Association, that tests every conceivable product and service on behalf of its members, from orange juice to luxury cars. Its reports are often critical of large influential companies. No company is allowed to reproduce a *Which?* report in its advertising.

Answers

caption 1 – picture E	caption 2 – picture G	caption 3 – picture D
caption 4 – picture F	caption 6 – picture C	caption 7 – picture B

Discussion ideas What notice do you take of 'consumer tests'? What are the advantages and shortcomings of such tests? Is there a similar magazine to *Which?* in your country? How well does it sell? What do you try to find out before you make an expensive purchase (of a hi-fi or a bike, for example)? Do you 'shop around' or go to the store with the widest range? Whose advice do you seek before purchasing?

7.4 Prepositions and particles   *Use of English*

Answers

1 of	2 in	3 on	4 to	5 by
6 in	7 with	8 in	9 of	10 since

11 in	12 to	13 of	14 on	15 of	16 by	17 out
18 in	19 to	20 between	21 around	22 for	23 on	

Discussion ideas What's your reaction to the new product? Are tobacco firms forced into selling new non-cigarette products in your country? Is there an anti-smoking campaign in your country? What form does it take and how effective is it? Are smokers discriminated against nowadays?

7.5 Idioms with GO   *Use of English*

Answers

2 His success in business seems to have gone to his head.
3 His shop has gone out of business after making heavy losses.
4 Trade has gone from bad to worse and staff are being laid off.
5 Supplies are so scarce that any models available are going for high prices.
6 By the time I opened the carton its contents had gone off.
7 I'll go over how it works before you try it yourself.
8 My new watch seems to have gone haywire, so I'd better take it back to the shop.
9 I was told it would be repaired free of charge, but the man in the shop has gone back on his promise.
10 When I bought it I thought it was a beautiful colour, but I've gone off it now.

11 The book was so popular that there weren't enough copies to go round.
12 Sales dropped before the Budget, but since then it has been going like a bomb.

7.6 Distorting the truth? *Questions and summary*

As the passage explains, the ASA is a consumer watchdog financed by the industry it controls. Its advertisements appear regularly in a wide range of newspapers and magazines.

Students should <u>underline</u> the vocabulary (question 1) and put a ⟨ring⟩ round the pronouns (question 2) as they occur in the passage.

Question 6, the summary, is quite demanding and will need some discussion and good note-making before complete paragraphs are written.

Answers

1 a handful – a small number of them   weakling – person with no strength   pledging – promising   akin – similar   ditch – small drainage channel   yardstick – standard of measurement   breach – break   unwittingly – without meaning to   monitor – watch   sceptical – disbelieving/doubtful   levy – small tax or compulsory payment

2 they (line 8) – advertisements   They (line 9) – unfair advertisements   us (line 29) – the ASA   it (line 50) – the walk   it (line 52) – the walk   they (line 75) – advertisers   they (line 78) – media owners   they (line 101) – the public   they (line 109) – challenged advertisers   them (line 111) – challenged advertisements   its (line 128) – the ASA's   this (line 133) – that the system of self control worked in the public's interest

3 make you into 15 stone he-man; take years off your life; riot of colour in just a few days; 5 minutes walk to the beach (if average walker would take longer); house overlooking ditch (described as a 'river')

4 asks advertisers for supporting evidence, or to amend the ad or withdraw it

5 chairman and most council members not allowed to have any involvement in advertising

6 complaints from public; 500 rules for advertisers; not TV and radio; unfair or misleading ads have to be amended or withdrawn; financed by levy; not influenced by advertisers; no legal powers (+ other points perhaps?)

7.7 Improving the customer's way of life *Listening*

The conversation, part of a broadcast (based on an article by Hilary Macaskill in *The Guardian*), contains a lot of information. There are two sets of questions: 1 to 8 to be answered on the first listening and 9 to 21 on the second.

Answers   1 14   2 lectures   3 English   4 some 5 greets everyone   6 very similar to Mitsukoshi   7 six days a week   8 each other 9 300   10 enhancing the quality   11 lunch bag   raw fish   rice 12 dream room for resting   13 bowler   flowers   gloves 14 play area   beer garden   15 railways   16 platform   train 17 10 to 6 or 6.30   18 transplanted   19 price   range of choice 20 service   quality   21 luggage   passports   relations accommodation

Transcript

Presenter: During her visit to the Far East recently Ingrid Fleming spent a day in Japan's largest department store, Mitsukoshi, and the oldest too, I believe, Ingrid?

Ingrid: Yes, that's right, Bill. Three hundred years ago it started as a simple kimono store and then it expanded. Now it's the largest department store chain in the Far East. Its main store is in downtown Tokyo and it has fourteen branches throughout Japan and fourteen associated stores and seven overseas stores.

Presenter: Is there even one in London?

Ingrid: Oh, yes.

Presenter: Er . . tell me, how is Mitsukoshi different from . . from, say, Harrods?

Ingrid: Well, they don't really aim to sell goods to satisfy everyday needs, like a supermarket. They hope to 'find ways of enhancing the quality of customers' lives'. Now, unlike Harrods, the main Mitsukoshi store has a theatre, it has a cinema, a museum, an art gallery. It offers concerts, lectures and classes. In fact, all the Japanese department stores are in the business of not just selling, but of improving the customers' way of life.

Presenter: And how do they set about this?

Ingrid: Well, one example: they have a Ladies Club with lectures and classes in education and in literature and in traditional arts and crafts, in painting, flower-arranging, calligraphy. And they have exhibitions – I saw one called 'The Life and Times of Queen Victoria' and there was one called 'The Gold of Peru' and another on Russian Romantic paintings. And then there's a theatre with its own staff shows and visiting troupes and traditional theatre and classical dance – everything like that. And . . and with the ticket you also get a lunch bag. In the lunch bag there's *sushi*, that's raw fish with rice and there's wine and sandwiches and a magazine, in case the show's a bit boring.

Presenter: Hahaha. What other facilities do they have?

Ingrid: Well, they'll look after your baby while you're shopping. They put

71

the baby in a 'dream room for resting babies'. And they arrange your wedding, they provide rooms for the ceremony and the reception. And there's a wide choice of restaurants: the main store even has an Italian and Chinese restaurant and a McDonald's.

Presenter: Oh. H . . how do they cater for their foreign visitors?

Ingrid: Well, they've been careful to provide brochures and store directory in English as well as in Japanese. If you say to someone . . er . . 'Do you speak English?' they smile at you and then they rush off to find somebody who does. At the information desk they don't just tell you where certain departments are, they ask . . they answer any question you want to ask. Oh, and one other thing I found lovely: in the lifts they have girls who announce what's on each floor in a sort of recitation, a sing-songy recitation, and they're dressed identically in a uniform of skirts with a waistcoat, a little bowler hat with flowers and beautiful little white gloves – just like dolls. And then as you come out of the lift or . . or as you step off the escalator there's a . . a girl whose job is simply to say 'Welcome!' Haha, it's wonderful, it's wonder . . oh, and they have racks of yellow umbrellas for customers to borrow to cross over to the annexe in rainy weather. Oh, it's amazing, it's wonderful. Oh and you have to go to the roof garden, there's a play area for children there and a beer garden with a view of the city.

Presenter: Er . . Mitsukoshi's the only store to have these though, I suppose?

Ingrid: Oh, no no no. You get the lift girls in . . in . . in every department store and . . you know, with different coloured uniforms and roof gardens too. Some stores even have their own railways.

Presenter: Have their own railways?

Ingrid: Mhm. They're built by one of the private commuter railway companies. Odakyu or Keio in Tokyo or Hanshin or Kintetsu in Osaka. You see, you take the lift to the basement and you step out onto the platform where your train is waiting. All the stores are huge, have at least eight floors and the most amazing variety of goods on offer, Japanese ones and imported ones.

Presenter: And when are these palaces open?

Ingrid: From 10 o'clock in the morning till 6 or 6.30 in the evening. And the restaurant floors are open later, till about 10.30 at night.

Presenter: Every day of the week?

Ingrid: No, they're closed on one day of the week, but they're open on Sundays and on national holidays when they're crowded with families of shoppers.

Presenter: Mm. What can we learn from the Japanese example, do you think?

Ingrid: Well, you see, I think the Japanese department store really is a feature of the Japanese way of life. I don't think it can be transplanted to the West. I mean, here stores compete in terms of price and range of choice. Now, in Japan the competition between the department stores is different, they compete on service and on quality. If you want discount prices there you . . you can go to a different type of store. You know, h . . here we shop around to find the cheapest prices. In Japan, people don't care about that so much. You see, if you . . well, to see how the idea can be transplanted to London, I think the best thing is to go to Mitsukoshi in Regent Street. You see, it's like stepping into a different world. The staff will spend hours and hours dealing with worried Japanese tourists who've lost their luggage or passports or can't find their relations in London or can't find accommodation. You know, it's wonderful but it's no way to compete with the prices of John Lewis's or Selfridges, you know, which are just round the corner in Oxford Street.

(Time: 5 minutes 30 seconds)

Presenter: Mm. Ingrid, many thanks for joining us.

Ingrid: Thank you, bye bye.

Discussion ideas

Are department stores in your country similar in any way to Japanese ones? What seems to be Ingrid Fleming's attitude to Japan: curious, patronising, chauvinistic? Describe your country's top department store.

7.8 Knowing your rights   *Listening*

Two goes will probably be necessary for students to get all the answers. Point out that in the exam they may not be able to get them all on the first listening, so they must learn not to panic or lose heart if things seem 'too quick' for them, but leave a gap and concentrate on the next question.

Answers

1 contract
2 merchantable   secondhand   fall apart
  purpose   seller
  described   large and juicy   tiny
3 Recommended: a) b) c)
4 obvious fault;   fault;   ignored   suitability;   ignored
  expert;   change your mind;   received   gift
5 If he's mistakenly priced an item too low. Or if he doesn't want to disturb window display.
6 As evidence of purchase and date of purchase (if you need to return the item).
7 Too costly for seller – cheaper to give you your money back.
8 Citizens' Advice Bureau   Trading Standards Office   Consumer Advice Centre

Transcript

Presenter: Many consumers are unaware of their rights in buying goods from shops and traders. John Scott of the Office of Fair Trading is here to explain exactly what your rights are under English law. John, first of all, what are the Acts that give the buyer rights?

John: Well, Barbara, there are two Acts: there's the Sale of Goods Act and the Trade Descriptions Act and both cover the rights of a buyer in contracts that he or she enters into with traders.

Presenter: And who are 'traders' exactly?

73

John: Well, 'traders' means any shop, doorstep salesman, street market or mail order firm.

Presenter: I see, and what is a 'contract' then in this respect?

John: Well, if you buy anything from a trader you have in fact entered into a contract with him.

Presenter: And . . er . . does the trader have obligations?

John: Yes, he has three main obligations. The first one is that the goods are 'of merchantable quality' . . .

Presenter: What does . . what does 'merchantable' mean then?

John: Well, that means 'fit for the purpose', bearing in mind the price that you've paid for it, the nature of the goods and how they're described. For example, a pair of shoes which fall apart after two weeks' normal wear are not of merchantable quality. Very cheap or secondhand goods needn't be top quality but they must still fulfil this obligation. And the second obligation is that the goods are 'fit for any particular purpose made known to the seller'.

Presenter: Could you give me an example of that?

John: Well, if you've asked the seller if the kitchen mixer you're being shown will be powerful enough to knead bread dough and he says it will, then he's entered into a contract, and if it breaks under the strain of your bread-making, you're entitled to a refund. And the third one is that the goods are 'as described'.

Presenter: Um . . do . . 'described on the package'?

John: Yes, on the package or as illustrated or described on a display sign or verbally by the seller himself. Er . . for example, a packet of frozen prawns which shows large juicy prawns on the outside and the ones inside are tiny, then you have cause for complaint. Or if the label says the blanket is pink and it turns out to be blue, then again you have a cause for complaint.

Presenter: And if you think you have a cause for complaint, what should you do?

John: Well, you must take the item back to the shop, unless it's too large or fragile to move, in which case the trader must collect it himself. And you'll be entitled to all or part of your money back, a cash refund, plus compensation for any loss or personal injury.

Presenter: I see, I . . I've sometimes been offered a credit note by the trader in that sort of situation.

John: Well, no, the buyer is under no obligation to accept a credit note but he or she may accept the offer of a replacement or a repair to the item or you can insist on a refund according to the law.

Presenter: Instead of taking it back to the shop, would it be a good idea to send it to the manufacturer?

John: No, definitely not. It's the retailer's responsibility. But you could sue the manufacturer if you've suffered personal injury, say.

Presenter: And . . um . . are there any exceptions to the requirement that the retailer should refund your money?

John: Yes, there are a few. You can't get your money back if you've examined the goods before you bought them and failed to notice any obvious fault. And also if you were told about any specific fault by the salesman at the time of purchase. And also if you ignored the seller's advice on the suitability of the product – if he said the mixer wasn't suitable for bread dough, for example. And also if you ignored the seller's claim that he wasn't expert enough to offer advice – I mean, if the glue you bought would be suitable for sticking metal to plastic, for example . . .

Presenter: I see, but . . what happens if you buy something and then you change your mind about it?

John: Ah, well, now once you've bought an item you can't legally change your mind about wanting it, but many shops do allow you to do this for the sake of goodwill.

Presenter: And .. er .. also, if you've had a .. something as a present .. um .. and it goes wrong?

John: Well, legally again the recipient of the gift really has no rights, it's the buyer who has the rights. Again, though, shops may not be too strict about this and the manufacturer's guarantee may cover you anyway.

Presenter: Can .. um .. can a shop-keeper refuse to sell you something? Are there any circumstances in which that could happen?

John: Oh yes. Yes, indeed. Shops don't have to sell you anything. If a retailer has made a mistake and priced an item too low, for example, or doesn't wish to disturb a window display he needn't sell you something.

Presenter: And w .. should one keep receipts or doesn't it matter if you throw them away?

John: Well, the .. the usefulness of keeping receipts is that you have some evidence of your purchase and also the date of purchase, which some-times is very important. But the re-tailer is not within his rights to say 'No refunds without a receipt'.

Presenter: Supposing a retailer refuses to give a refund?

John: Well, in that case you should go to your local Citizens' Advice Bureau or Trading Standards Office and that's sometimes called 'Consumer Advice Centre'.

Presenter: Can you .. how .. how could I find out where these places are?

John: Well, you could find the address in the phone book in fact.

Presenter: I .. I see. And if the worst comes to the worst?

John: Well, you may have to go to court and sue the seller for your money or for compensation. But that's very rare, I'm glad to say, as it's more costly for a retailer to defend himself in court than to give you your money back.

Presenter: John, thank you very much.

John: Thank you.

(Time: 4 minutes 55 seconds)

Discussion ideas   How is the consumer protected in your country by the law? What advice would you give to a dissatisfied customer about returning goods? Do consumers get enough protection in your country? What organisations exist to stand up for their rights?

7.9   Advertisements   *Picture conversation*

Student A looks at activity 13, which shows the pictorial part of an ad for the American Express Card together with the text of an ad for the British Telecom Radiopager. Student B looks at activity 51, which shows the pictorial part of the Radiopager ad together with the text of the American Express one. Each student has questions to ask the other and later has to explain how the text fits with the pictures.

This is, as you can see, quite an elaborate communication activity, so

75

make sure that everyone follows the instructions given in activities 13 and 51.

7.10   Shopping in Moscow   *Communication activity*

Student A looks at activity 14, where there is part of a newspaper article about the difficulties of shopping in Moscow. Student B looks at 52, where the rest of the same article is printed. The idea is to complete the 'jigsaw' by paraphrasing the information in their own words. (If any students might be offended by the main theme, the non-availability of toilet paper, you could substitute another article cut up into two parts with one for each partner. However, as the article is a UPI report it is in the best possible taste!)

7.11   Writing a balanced, relevant essay   *Composition*

The emphasis in the discussion, note-making and writing should be on creating an essay that gives equal prominence to the pros and to the cons. The list of points in the Student's Book is by no means exhaustive and deliberately contains several points that are of less relevance than others – it should be treated as a starting point, therefore.

Point out that a good essay should contain PRECISE AND APPROPRIATE VOCABULARY. This does not mean using the longest words that come to mind, but it does often mean using words that are unambiguous and suitable for the fairly formal style of an essay. Words like 'nice', 'good', 'bad', 'beautiful' or 'boring' should be avoided, perhaps? In marking the completed essays, watch out for this and suggest alternative vocabulary items when necessary. This is not something that can be 'taught' in class – it has to be absorbed through reading and experimentation in use.

8 Books

(Perhaps begin with listening exercise 8.8.)

8.1 Vocabulary

Perhaps start by finding out what kinds of books the members of the class normally read for pleasure, in their own language as well as in English. Do they count reading as one of their leisure interests, or are they 'too busy' to get much reading done?

Answers

1 prose   2 creative   3 accessible
4 figure of speech   5 simile   6 metaphor
7 imagery   8 alliteration   9 hyperbole   10 paradox
11 allegory   12 message   13 characterisation   14 satirical
15 classic
16 thrillers, whodunits, best-sellers   17 dustjacket, contents, blurb
18 foreword, preface, dedication   19 collection, book, anthology
20 dissect, study, analyse   21 involved, complex, intricate
22 struggle, wade, get   23 well-written, thought-provoking, readable
24 symbolically, metaphorically, figuratively   25 dreams, illusion, the imagination

Discussion ideas

(See above.) If you get too high-brow in discussing literature, you may lose some of the class. It's advisable, therefore, to give everyone an opportunity to talk about the books they enjoy reading, even if they 'only' read thrillers or romantic novels. That's why this unit is entitled *Books* and not 'Literature'.

What's your favourite book? What do you like about it? What book has had the greatest influence on you and your way of looking at things? Can a book 'change your life' as blurbs often claim?
(More discussion on this theme in 8.10.)

1 is from *The Grapes of Wrath*, John Steinbeck's best-known novel, which describes the story of a family of dispossessed farmers driven off their land in Oklahoma and forced to search for a land of plenty in California, but not to find it there. Steinbeck, who was awarded the Nobel Prize for Literature in 1962, is also the author of *Cannery Row*, *Of Mice and Men*, and *East of Eden*.

2 is from *The Mosquito Coast* by Paul Theroux, the story of a family who abandon civilisation and go to live in the Honduran jungle, which they hope will be a paradise. Their life there becomes a nightmare. The novel is a compelling creation of an obsessive central character ('Father') and his struggle to become master of his self-created world. Paul Theroux is also the author of *The Family Arsenal*, *Picture Palace* and *Saint Jack*, as well as accounts of his travels in *The Great Railway Bazaar*, *The Old Patagonian Express* and *Kingdom by the Sea*.

3 is from *A Farewell to Arms* by Ernest Hemingway, the story of a love affair set against the background of the First World War. Hemingway, whose deceptively simple style sets him apart from other 'serious' writers, won the Nobel Prize for Literature in 1954. His other famous novels include *For Whom the Bell Tolls*, *The Old Man and the Sea* and *Across the River and into the Trees*. His short stories are also highly regarded and accessible.

By presenting the opening paragraphs of the novels, I hope to whet students' appetites to read more of the authors concerned – for their pleasure as well as to improve their English.

The questions are open-ended and should be discussed. The answers are suggestions and you, or your students, may disagree with some of them.

Answers

1 Extract no. 1: 'May . . . June', 'day after day' 'every day'; the changing weather; the growth of green weeds and their subsequent 'fraying' and dying back

2 Extract no. 3: 'Troops went by the house and down the road', 'the leaves fell', 'troops marching', 'troops marching under the window and guns going past'; the use of prepositions and particles: *across*, *along*, *past*, etc.

3 Extract no. 2: 'savages', 'awfulness', 'dope-taking, door-locking, ulcerated danger-zone of rabid scavengers . . .'; a piling-up of words that suggest decay and violence

4 (see above)

5 Extract no. 3 (Hemingway)

6   Extract no. 1 (Steinbeck) – or Extract no. 3?
7   Extract no. 2 (Theroux)
8   Extract no. 1 – and Extract no. 3?
9   (for discussion)
10 (see above)

8.3   Three British novels   *Reading*

Background   1 is from *Midnight's Children* by Salman Rushdie,
                    an Indian writer who lives in Britain. The book is a
fascinating, magical family saga set against the historical events of 20th
century India. In the story the narrator is one of the 1,001 children born at
midnight on the day of India's independence, all of whom are endowed with
extraordinary talents or powers. India has a unique position in the British
imagination, seeming to evoke nostalgia and the lure of the exotic, reflected
in the success of novels and films about the British in India before 1947 (eg
Paul Scott's *The Raj Quartet* and E. M. Forster's *A Passage to India*).
Midnight's Children was awarded the prestigious Booker Prize in 1981.
Salman Rushdie is also the author of *Shame*, set in Pakistan.

2 is from *The Affirmation* by Christopher Priest, a haunting story of a
man who is two people, one of whom lives in another imagined world –
more convincing than the 'real' world. All of Priest's works have a strong
element of fantasy and are set in the future or in a dream world or relate
reality to a disconcerting unreal world. His other books include *A Dream of
Wessex* and *The Glamour*.

3 is from *The Millstone* by Margaret Drabble, the story of a girl who has
an illegitimate child. The story, narrated with wry humour by Rosamund
herself, describes a time of emotional transition and the hardships of dealing
with unmarried motherhood. Margaret Drabble's other books include
Jerusalem the Golden (see exercise 3.4), *The Waterfall*, *The Needle's Eye*,
The Realms of Gold and *The Ice Age*.

Again, I hope to whet students' appetites for further reading, though
Midnight's Children is probably unsuitable for linguistic (and even cultural)
reasons.

The answers given below are suggestions and you, or your students, may
disagree with some of them.

Answers

1   Extract no. 2
2   Extract no. 1
3   Extract no. 3
4   Confusion, lack of organisation; incomplete sentences ('No, that won't

do', 'it's important to be more . . .'); narrator talking to himself ('spell it out'); short sentences ('There were gasps', 'The time matters, too')

5   Obsession with truth, certainty; 'words' repeated, 'choose', 'choices'; beginning again

6   Light-heartedness, humour ('an age appropriate for such adventures', 'I do remember rightly', 'we had conceived our plan'); the description of the meticulous plans

7   Saleem Sinai: self-important, comic (?)   Peter Sinclair: pompous, obsessive   Rosamund: self-deprecating, amusing, self-mocking

8   'Clock-hands joined palms', 'saluting clocks', 'handcuffed to history'

9   'I once thought . . .', 'I have since learned . . .', 'all prose is a form of deception'

10 'If I remember rightly . . . I do remember rightly', 'wearing a gold curtain ring on the relevant finger', 'having read . . . a good deal of cheap fiction', 'carried ourselves with considerable aplomb'

11 (for discussion)

12 (for discussion)

13 All have first person narrators; all use self-correction as a narrative device

8.4 Conditional sentences   *Use of English*

Answers

2   If he didn't always have his nose in a book he might (sometimes) pay attention to what I say.

3   Had I known that he was the author, I wouldn't have been so rude about his new book.

4   Should you wish to keep the book any longer, please let me know.

5   If it hadn't been/wasn't/weren't such a readable book, I wouldn't have been able to get through it so quickly.

6   If I had had enough money with me, I would have been able to buy the books I wanted.

7   If you've read the first chapter, you'll never be able to put it down.

8   If it isn't in stock, we can order it for you.

9   Were I to meet the author one day, I'd ask him to sign my copy of this book.

10 If the book had not contained such explicit descriptions of sex and violence, it would not have become an immediate best-seller.

11 If picaresque novels were fashionable/more fashionable, he might/ would be able to get his new book published.

12 If there's a book you've really enjoyed reading, recommend it to your class-mates.

8.5 Linking words and phrases   *Use of English*

If your class finds this too difficult, write up the missing words and phrases on the board, arranged at random. (Use the first answer suggested below in each case.) Ask anyone who knows something about each author to say a little about him or her.

Answers

1 for example/such as/for instance/particularly
2 consequently/so/and   3 namely/that is to say   4 moreover/what is more/yet   5 in particular/above all
6 although/even though/and yet   7 nonetheless/nevertheless/moreover
8 by comparison/by contrast/on the other hand   9 at least/at any rate
10 in other words/that is to say

8.6 Writing fiction   *Questions and summary*

Background

The French Lieutenant's Woman is John Fowles' best-known book. It was published in 1969 and made into a film in 1980. The book itself is an elaborate piece of Victorian-style narrative, combined with modern psychological and historical insights. It is full of stylistic tricks, many of which are difficult to appreciate on the first reading. John Fowles is also the author of *The Collector*, *The Magus*, *Daniel Martin* and *A Maggot*.

Answers

1 countless different reasons (see lines 3 to 10)
2 characters and events develop lives of their own; a planned world is a dead world
3 they are autonomous; they exist within their own world
4 to be able to choose what they are to do
5 Victorian author-narrator: omniscient and decreeing
   modern author-narrator: belief in freedom
6 of being deluded, insincere, dishonest (?)
7 We believe we control our children, colleagues, ourselves; we fictionalise our own pasts – make the past more interesting, exciting, honourable, reprehensible, logical; we daydream about what we'll do in the future, how we'll behave – this influences the way we actually do behave when the time comes.

Discussion ideas

Perhaps look more closely at the style of the passage. What is meant, for example, by the 'as . . . like . . .' images in lines 5 to 7? What are the words the author puts

81

into the reader's mouth? Given that this is a digression in the ongoing narrative of the novel, does it seem relevant or interesting?

8.7 The novels of William Wharton *Listening*

As this recorded broadcast is rather long, you may wish to save time by pausing the tape between the description of each book to give students time to write down (and perhaps compare) their answers to each set of questions. Suitable places for pausing are indicated in the transcript below.

Answers

1 Birdy's friend, Al   2 Birdie   3 as if thoughts being formed as you read them
4 grandson and son of 'Dad' (but John is, of course, Billy's 'Dad')
5 Three: John, Billy and Dad (?)   6 downtrodden husband and factory worker; farmer with young family on small farm   7 by watching TV
8 very intelligent – best bridge players and poets in the army
9 real name: Will Knott – will not – won't – Wont: nickname
10 everything is happening as you read it
11 build 'nests' – fixing up rented rooms   12 to seek the answers to the big questions (!)   13 impression of untidy, unarranged experience
14 *A Midnight Clear*   15 *Dad*

Transcript

Presenter: Gillian Pike has been looking at the novels of the American writer, William Wharton, whose first novel came out in 1978 I believe, Gillian?

Gillian: Yes, that's right, Douglas. In fact, he was already middle-aged when he wrote this first novel, which is called *Birdy*. Um . . he spent his younger years as a painter.

Presenter: W . . tell us about *Birdy*.

Gillian: *Birdy* i . . is about a boy who dreams of being able to fly, he . . um . . he keeps canaries and he imagines himself being as good as them. The story is told through the voice of his friend Al and it's interspersed with the thoughts of Birdy himself. The starting point is from the point where Birdy is a patient in a military psychiatric hospital, apparently believing himself to be a canary. And we see how he grows up through boyhood and adolescence obsessed with

his canaries and with the desire to learn to fly. He trains . . haha . . he trains by flapping his arms and . . and learning to sing like his canaries. And he has a favourite, called Birdie, but that's spelt with an IE – a female that is. I . . it does sound ludicrous, I know, but it is told in an utterly convincing way, all in the present tense . . a . . a . . as if the thoughts are being formed at the moment of your reading them. It's . . it has a very immediate quality. I suppose its theme is . . . madness and obsession.

Presenter: I see, and his second novel and probably, I suppose, the best well-known is *Dad*, which was published in 1981, wasn't it?

Gillian: Yes, and I think this is his most substantial work to date. It's a powerful and moving book. 'Dad' is the grandfather of Billy, whose own father John tells how he's recalled from France to look after his mother, who's had a heart attack. Then Dad himself becomes ill, but mentally ill. He's eventually diagnosed as a 'successful schizophrenic' – that's someone who's been living two lives all his life. In this case one life as the downtrodden husband and factory worker in Los Angeles, which is what he actually is, and the other in his imagination as a farmer with a young family on a small farm near the East Coast. The story in this case is narrated from the son's point of view partly, and partly from *his* son's (Billy's) point of view as they drive across America from California to Philadelphia – and with snatches of the grandfather's thoughts in his fantasy world.

Presenter: I see, and what exactly is the theme of the book?

Gillian: Well, the book is . . is really about relationships . . um . . relationships between married people and between parents and children. It . . it's also about illness, about growing old and dying. And, as is common in many of Wharton's novels, about escaping from an unhappy reality. Um . . Dad, for instance, lives in another idyllic world and his domineering wife escapes from her fears by watching TV. It's actually . . it's a wonderful book, it carries you along remorselessly and it completely drains the emotions.

Presenter: Mm, and . . er . . *A Midnight Clear*, which came out in 1982, how do you rate that?

Gillian: W . . well, again, it's a remarkable book but it's . . it's less substantial than *Dad*. Um . . but it's . . it's moving and . . and gripping. It's . . it's about six young soldiers, who are part of the US Army Intelligence Corps, who are sent to a lonely château in the snowy Ardennes Forest at Christmas 1944. They're . . they're iconoclastic, very young, very intelligent – 'the best

bridge players and best poets in the US Army'. And . . and they come across a squad of elderly German soldiers, who want to surrender, and they make plans for . . for capturing them and are about to do so when the battle starts to rage over them and th . . everything goes wrong. Some escape and some are killed or wounded.

Presenter: Mm, I see, and . . er . . the theme?

Gillian: Well, the theme is of course the stupidity of war, the senseless killing of gifted young men and also about the . . the confusion of incompetence and bad luck. The . . the story's told from the point of view of the 19-year-old sergeant, known by the nickname 'Wont' – well, his real name is Will Knott, you know, that's spelt K N O TT. Again i . . in the present tense and i . . it's as if everything is happening as you read it.

Presenter: Now, 1984 saw the publication of *The Scumbler*, that's a curious title, w . . what does it refer to?

Gillian: Ah, well, 'scumbling' is a technique used in painting. It's a sort of . . well, it's . . it's a sel . . it's a selective overlaying of paint on parts of a picture, which change the image. The narrator calls himself 'the Scumbler' . . er . . he's in his sixties and is a painter who lives in Paris with his wife Kate and their five kids. When he's not painting he rents rooms and fixes them as 'nests' or places where he can escape. Eventually he decides to go to Spain to sort of, well, to 'seek the answers to the big questions in life'. The . . the narrative style of William Wharton here has the effect of giving the impression of a . . untidy, unarranged experience without the . . the tidying-up effects that the . . um . . that past tense narration usually gives. It's . . it's very distinctive and I find it wonderful.

Presenter: Mm, and of all his books, I suppose that *A Midnight Clear* is the most easily approachable, would you agree with that?

Gillian: I suppose so, but . . but as I said . . a . . *Dad* is by far the most interesting. Er . . best of all, read all four. You won't regret it.

(Time: 6 minutes 10 seconds)

Discussion ideas   Look at the extract from *Dad* in the Student's Book. How would you characterise the style? What other books have you read that are told in the present tense? What seems attractive/unattractive to you about the novels described?

8.8 How to write a best-seller   *Listening*

The questions on this recording should be attempted in two goes, as suggested in the Student's Book.

Answers

1 something else   (round-the-world yachtswoman and broadcaster)
2 well-known author   'trusted'   (romantic novels   thrillers   sex and intrigue)
3 sex and violence, intrigue, action, romance   (humour   science fiction   the detective story)
4 non-fiction   in fashion   (keeping fit   dieting   running)
5 TV series   scripts   (plug   repeated)
6 book   film   film   book   (after   instead of)
7 interviews   TV   signing copies
8 TV mini-series   (successful   ridiculous   worthy)
9 long   carelessly and quickly   track   (established)
10 publishing   evaluated   part-time, underpaid

Transcript

Presenter: If you've ever felt you want to give up your job and write that best-selling novel, then perhaps you should listen to author Julian Morrison's advice. He's been looking at the ingredients of the best-seller. Julian?

Julian: Well, first of all what is a best-seller? Well, I'm talking about books that sell over half a million copies in paperback in the UK plus some sales in the USA and in translation overseas. So, how to get started? Well, first of all, there's no doubt it's a great help to be famous for something else already. Clare Francis, the round-the-world yachtswoman, had enormous success with her first novel *Night Sky* and that was simply on the strength of her books describing her sailing and her fame as a broadcaster. Secondly, you're half way there if you're a well-known author already with your own distinctive style and . . and formula: 'Have you read the new Jeffrey Archer?', 'I . . I must get the new Frederick Forsyth', people say to each other. And it doesn't seem to matter if the new one is inferior to the others, it'll still sell well. And there are a couple of dozen writers who are 'trusted' in this way. If you like romance, then you know the new Danielle Steele will suit you a . . and the new Barbara Cartland, of course, we mustn't forget Barbara. Er . . if you enjoy straightforward thrillers, Alistair Maclean is your cup of tea. If you want sex and intrigue, then Judith Krantz or Jackie Collins. The third point is: you must make sure you include a mixture of the very essential ingredients. Sex and violence, of course, intrigue . . er . . action, romance are constantly in fashion. Other ingredients are perhaps less easy to . . to control. Er . . humour: you can have humour but it should have some kind of novelty too. Er . . science fiction, well, that's a speciality interest only at the moment . . er . . the detective story . . mm . . that's out of fashion now, although Mrs Christie is still very much in demand. Ah . . fourthly, you could try to write a non-fiction book on a theme currently in fashion. Books on keeping fit or dieting have been selling well. Last year it was running that was all the go. OK . . er . . five . . er . . if you're lucky enough to have your own TV series . . er . . you can write a book from your scripts. *Indian Cookery, Vegetarian Cookery, Chinese Cookery* . . er . . b . . b . . *Life on Earth, The Living Planet* – that sort of thing. And here you have the added advantage that you can plug your book at the end of each programme and then . . then there's always the possibility of a repeat of the series and therefore more sales of more books. And the sixth point I'd like to . . er . . make is: if you can write a book of a film – or better still have a film made of *your* book. Er . . *Terms of Endearment* the novel was very little known until the film came out. Erm . . *Indiana Jones and the Temple of Doom*. Er . . for some people . . for some

reason people will want to read the book after they've seen the film or perhaps buy the book instead of seeing the film, although quite often they're very different, of course. Oh, and it's a great help to have 'Soon a major movie' on the cover. Er . . the seventh point: having written your book you must be prepared to tour the country and the USA giving interviews, appearing on TV shows and signing copies of your book. This self-publicity is essential unless you're already terribly famous, although even the well-known are not averse to appearing on the top talk shows to give their book a little boost. Um . . eight: well now, to get more sales of a previous year's best-seller have a TV mini-series made of it. Haha . . amazingly enough people seem to want to relive the experience of a dreadful TV series by reading the book immediately after. Shirley Conran's amazingly successful and quite ridiculous book about a soft porn star *Lace*, for instance. Judith Krantz's *Princess Daisy* . . er . . w . . w . . John Le Carré's *Smiley's People*, a perhaps more worthy example. Er . . the ninth point I'd like to make is: unless you're already famous, your book should be very long, say 500 pages, and easy to read in the sense that the reader can read it very carelessly and quickly and still keep track of the plot. But if you fancy yourself as a 'literary' writer, then don't expect to be able to write a best-seller. Um . . unless you win a prize. For example the winner and runners-up of the yearly Booker Prize can expect to sell very well . . mm . . possibly another three . . to . . thousand to five thousand copies, even if they are quite literary. But nothing like on the scale of the established best-selling authors like Wilbur Smith, Jack Higgins or . . or Robert Ludlum. Er . . the tenth point: it is of enormous help to have lots of friends who are in publishing. Publishers get inundated with hundreds of unsolicited manuscripts each week and they send them off to poor, underpaid, part-time readers to evaluate and it's their judgement that decides if a new author is going to sell or not. If you're already well-known, you have a much better chance. So, finally, returning to my first points, the best and most sure-fire way of getting a book in the best-seller list is to be famous already. So if you're not, then it's going to be a big gamble. However good your writing is and however sensational your plot!

(Time: 5 minutes 45 seconds)

Discussion ideas Has anyone read any of the authors or books referred to? Get them to tell the rest of the class about them. Talk about a current best-seller that many of the class have read or at least heard of: it needn't be an English or American one. What kind of books are best-sellers in your country? Do you scorn best-sellers or enjoy them?

8.9   Up the Garden Path   *Pronunciation*

Each student has a different extract from Sue Limb's hilarious novel *Up the Garden Path* (1984). Student A has the beginning of chapter 1 in activity 15, student B the beginning of chapter 4 in activity 53 and student C the beginning of chapter 8 in activity 74. As well as reading the extracts clearly and 'with feeling', they should speculate about the story that connects them and discuss what they have found out about Izzy and Maria.

These are quite long passages and there should be time for you to listen to most of the class and give advice on individual pronunciation problems. Suggest that they work on eradicating persistent errors on their own – by recording their voices on a cassette recorder at home, for example.

8.10   What did you enjoy?   *Communication activity*

Here, for the first time perhaps, students are given an opportunity to discuss the 'prescribed book' they have been asked to read for the Proficiency exam. Working in groups of three they should all look at the questions in activity 55.

If, however, none of the books seem suitable for your class (or if you're 'against' this option), there are questions in activity 12 on students' general reading, to be discussed in groups of three.

8.11   Writing about a book   *Composition*

Here, again, students can deal with a prescribed book *or* with another book they have enjoyed. For the first time, however, they are asked to limit themselves to just 350 words, following the advice in the Student's Book. Preliminary discussion and notes are essential. Also students should decide what their opening and closing sentences are going to be before they begin writing.

Point out the need for A GOOD CONCLUSION to a composition. What is the function of a conclusion? What is it supposed to leave the reader with? Is it the final paragraph or just the final sentence that is most important in leaving the reader with the desired impression? Are there any useful multi-purpose final sentences that anyone can suggest? Before collecting the completed compositions for marking, get the members of the class to look at each other's conclusions and comment on them (helpfully or kindly).

9 Politics

(Perhaps begin with listening exercise 9.8.)

9.1 Vocabulary

Perhaps start by getting members of the class to declare their political allegiances – if they could vote or do vote, who do they vote for? If they are apolitical or anti-political, get them to explain why. (If politics is a sensitive subject for your students, don't begin like this!)

Answers
1 Senate Congress 2 constitutional monarchy 3 referendum 4 corruption
5 constituency 6 appointed 7 reshuffle 8 Budget
9 Treasury 10 upper lower chamber 11 reactionary
12 radical 13 moderate 14 embassy 15 consulate
16 protest against, demonstrate against, oppose 17 coup, revolution, uprising 18 collapse, defeat, overthrow 19 freedom fighters, guerrillas, revolutionaries 20 foreign agent, spy, traitor
21 chauvinism, jingoism, nationalism 22 platform, policy, programme
23 leader, councillor, mayor 24 bureaucracy, officialdom, red tape
25 finance government spending, provide essential public services, redistribute wealth

Discussion ideas (See above.) How much do people in your country trust politicians? Are MPs and ministers respected people in your society? Is politics a common topic of conversation among your circle of friends, or does it tend to be avoided? How important is politics? Does it affect every aspect of one's life, as many Marxists would assert?

9.2 Andorra   *Reading*

It may be helpful to show students where Andorra is on a globe or a map, if – like most English people – they've never heard of the country. The article appeared in *The Guardian* in 1981, so – like any article about political events – it is 'out of date' by now. By the time you read this, the political situation in Andorra will undoubtedly have changed, but this doesn't matter if the article seems interesting.

Note that some of the answers below are debatable, to give the class a chance to discuss and justify their answers. Indeed they – or you – may disagree with the answers given.

Answers

1 miserably damp valleys – lovely snow a few hundred feet higher up; stuck between France and Spain up in the Pyrenees
2 free postal service; no schooling after 11 years; no army; no political parties
3 the Andorrans and their rulers (?)
4 the co-lords
5 no secondary schools
6 their political situation is stable (?)
7 not responded to the request
8 free elections   a police force   free postage   a working class
9 there's a lot of unforeseen trouble inside Andorra (well, that's an exaggeration – so the title is ironical)
The writer's attitude: amused, but not frivolous, curiosity

Discussion ideas   (See Student's Book.) Does anyone in the class have experience of another small, politically unusual country (Liechtenstein, Monaco, San Marino, The Vatican, Luxembourg (?) etc.)? Or of any regions in their country with unusual autonomous rights (Catalonia, West Berlin, etc.)? What would it be like to live in such places? How does your own country differ from Andorra in its political and cultural quirks?

9.3   Tired and emotional MPs   *Reading*

Perhaps point out that the expression *tired and emotional* (a euphemism for *drunk*) was coined by the British satirical magazine *Private Eye*, to avoid getting sued for libel. Hugh Gaitskell was Leader of the Opposition and leader of the Labour Party from 1955 until his death in 1963.

Answers

True: 2 3 4 5 9 (?) 16 17 20
False: 1 6 7 8 10 11 12 13 14 15 18 19
Attitudes: a blend of seriousness (or mock-seriousness?) and irreverence

Could a similar speech have been made in your country about a respected former politician? Would such an article have been written about it? Do you take the articles seriously? Is alcohol abuse a serious problem among young people in your country, or among politicians?

9.4 Collocations *Use of English*

The missing words are vocabulary items which can be worked out from the context. If your students find this too hard, you could read the whole article out to them with the gaps filled before they do the exercise. The first answer given in each case is the one used in the original article.

Answers

1 states   2 startlingly/shockingly/ridiculously
3 indicated/showed/expressed   4 astonishing/remarkable/startling   5 lake/surplus   6 amounted   7 around/about/under   8 elicited/obtained   9 dedicated/fervent/committed   10 statement   11 question/issue   12 undermine/harm   13 wine/booze/plonk

Discussion ideas   For European students: How do you feel about the EEC and its agricultural policies? Is the EEC a good thing for your country or a bad thing?

9.5 Idioms with COME *Use of English*

Answers

1   The Tories came into power in 1979.
2   The opposition came out against the proposal.
3   In the election for a new party leader the favourite came out on top.
4   The government has come in for a lot of criticism.
5   It's hard to/I can't come to terms with the government's defence policy.
6   My worst fears about this government have come true.
7   After retiring in 1980 he has decided to make a comeback to the political scene.
8   She's an up-and-coming young backbencher.
9   The situation has come to the boil now that that the government has to face a vote of confidence.
10 The tax cuts announced in the Budget do not come into effect until next year.

90

11 The miners came out on strike against the government's privatisation plans.

12 The government has come out badly in the recent public opinion polls.

9.6 A party conference   *Questions and summary*

Background   Information about the British SDP is given in the Student's Book. The passage, though by now dated and even then rather parochial in appeal, is nevertheless a typical piece of party conference reporting.

The Guardian was taken in by Ann Brennan's performance (see below). She is in fact *Mrs* Brennan, a 43-year-old taxi-driver's wife with a 24-year-old son ...

8 30 WORLD IN ACTION. Dr Max Atkinson, an Oxford academic, claims that most of the applause which punctuates a public speech is the result of a small number of oratorical tricks. And what Mrs Thatcher has been coached to do can equally be taught to many others. So he took in hand Ann Brennan, the wife of a London taxi driver who had never made a public speech in her life, but who was to attend the SDP conference at Buxton. She told Joe Haines, now of the Mirror but once speech writer to Harold Wilson when he was prime minister, what she wished to say, and Haines wrote her speech. The voice coach of the Royal Shakespeare Company taught Ann how to deliver it. Dr Atkinson showed her videos of the best clap-trapping devices. And before you could say Pygmalion, Ann was taking the conference by storm and being hailed by TV and the press (excluding, of course, the Mirror). Altogether a fascinating insight into the mechanics of manipulation.

Answers

1 Come off it – Don't be foolish, you're wrong   a one-man band – an organisation controlled and run by one person   unilaterally – without getting the other's agreement, independently   off the cuff – without notes   standing ovation – everyone in the audience on their feet clapping

2 media phrase used by Dr Owen's enemies; his self-confidence in running the party in his way and insisting on its independence
3 provoke ideas; challenge the members; be challenged by the members
4 too many graduates in the party; no appeal to the working class; need to attract more than middle-class voters if they want to win an election
5 not a one-man band; not trying to impose his views; no loss of influence after alliance with Liberals; flattering tributes to various party leaders and members; Alliance will be attractive to voters

Discussion ideas   Is there a similar party in your country to the SDP? Or are there many different parties? What sections of society in your country does each party draw its support from? Who is the 'best speaker' among the politicians in your country? What makes his or her speeches effective, do you think?

9.7   Taxes, taxes and more taxes   *Listening*

In the UK the Rates may have been replaced or supplemented by a poll tax, by the time you read this.

Answers

UK CENTRAL GOVERNMENT INCOME –
1 Income tax   Corporation tax   2 VAT   Excise duty   Customs duty
Road Fund Licence   3 Social Security
UK CENTRAL GOVERNMENT EXPENDITURE –
1 pensions   2 Unemployment   3 Social Security
4 National Health Service
UK LOCAL AUTHORITIES (ie Counties and Boroughs) INCOME –
1 Rates
UK LOCAL AUTHORITIES EXPENDITURE –
1 Education   2 Road   3 Housing

US FEDERAL GOVERNMENT INCOME – 1 Income   2 Corporation
3 Excise   4 Customs   5 Social Security
US FEDERAL GOVERNMENT EXPENDITURE –
1 Pensions   2 Social Security   3 Unemployment benefits
4 Food stamps   5 Defence
US INDIVIDUAL STATES INCOME – 1 Income   2 Sales
US INDIVIDUAL STATES EXPENDITURE –
1 Education   2 Road   3 Housing

UK 42%   US 33%
48% in France   28% in Japan   20% in Spain

92

Transcript

Presenter: We are hearing more and more in the West about governments attempting to reduce taxes by reducing public expenditure. But just what are taxes? As Eric Gardiner reports, it's not just income tax that's involved, and the costs which bite into the public purse may not all be the things we're willing to do without.

Eric: That's right, Mary. Well now, let's compare the way in which the public foots the bill for services in the UK and in the USA. First of all, let's take the UK. Now, there are three main sources of government income on a national level. There are taxes on income, that's Income Tax and Corporation Tax, which includes the Petroleum Revenue Tax on oil companies. And then there are taxes on expenditure, that's VAT and Excise Duty on alcohol, tobacco and petrol, and that includes Customs Duty on certain imports and the Road Fund Licence and other licence fees. And then there are Social Security contributions. Now, all the revenue the government receives is put into one big 'pot', which is called the Consolidated Fund, and that's to be redistributed as the Chancellor of the Exchequer, that's the man in charge of the Treasury, how he thinks fit. Now top of the list are Old-age Pensions, then Unemployment Benefits and Social Security benefits, as well as the National Health Service. And also very significant is the money that we spend on defence. And the government also foots the bill for part of the nation's costs on education, and road building and also public housing. Now local authorities, that's the counties and boroughs, they're responsible for spending on education and road building and public housing

as well. And part of the revenue for these is raised by means of the rates. Now, the rates are local property taxes based on the value and size of a house or flat. And these rates also pay for all the local services provided by the council.

Now in America, Federal Government is responsible for spending on pensions and social security and also unemployment benefits and then there are food stamps and defence – now defence in America represents 25% of total Federal Government expenditure. And all this revenue is raised by income taxes, corporation taxes, excise duties and customs duties and also by social security contributions. Now, the individual states levy their own income taxes and also sales taxes on retail goods and they use this revenue to pay for education, road construction, and other public works like public housing a . . and public services. And for every dollar that an American citizen pays to the Federal government, he pays 50 cents to the state. And whereas only 33% of America's Gross National Product goes in taxes, 42% of the UK's GNP goes in taxes. And if you want to compare other countries: Norway has 59% of its GNP, France 48%, Japan 28% and Spain 20%. And the higher the ratio, the better the social services offered by the State or more expensive the defence forces. So, you make a choice: if you want the poor and needy and the elderly to be looked after by the State rather than by their friends and relatives, then your taxes have to be high. And lower taxes mean restricted public services and less care for the less well-off, or the less hardy members of society.

(Time: 3 minutes 50 seconds)

Discussion ideas   What is your reaction to the last points made by the speaker? Are people in your country taxed too highly? Is too much public money spent on defence? Is enough spent on education, the dole and social services? How does the taxation system in your country compare with that of the UK and USA?

9.8   Her Majesty's Government   *Listening*

The guide's speech, simplified for his audience, may need to be amplified by you if students ask any questions about, for example, how a Bill becomes an Act, or how the principle of collective responsibility applies to Cabinet decisions, or what powers a Prime Minister has to take decisions independently of Parliament.

Answers   a) Westminster   b) Lords   c) Lord Chancellor   d) Commons   e) 635
f) non-party Speaker   g) regulating the life of the community
h) scrutinise   i) Whitehall   j) majority (party)   k) Secretaries of State   l) Ministers   m) MPs or peers   n) non-party professional
o) Forces   p) professional   q) Corporations   r) British Rail
s) the Post Office   t) Lord Chancellor   u) administration
v) justice   w) Parliament   x) Government   y) England and Wales   z) Scotland

Transcript

Guide: Er . . if you could all gather round here . . er . . just for a second please, because I'd like to explain a little about our system of government. Now there are three parts to the government of the United Kingdom and they are: legislature, executive and judiciary. Let's take legislature first, this is the law-making body of the State. Er . . now this is headed by the Monarch and includes the House of Lords and the House of Commons. The House of Lords consists of Peers of the Realm, now these are made life peers . . er . . usually in recognition for some public service or else they have succeeded to their titles by hereditary means and they are all presided over by the Lord Chancellor, who also happens to be the head of the judici-

ary in England and Wales. The House of Commons is composed of 635 Members of Parliament, elected by public ballot, ostensibly for a period of five years, and they are presided over by a non-party Speaker, who is chosen by the House. The duties of Parliament are: firstly, to pass laws regulating the life of the community, and secondly to scrutinise government policy and administration. Now on to the executive branch of government. This is headed by the Prime Minister, the Monarch's 'first minister', who's the leader of the majority party in the House of Commons. Now from her or his supporters the Prime Minister will choose a Cabinet of approximately 20 Secretaries of State and Ministers. Then we have the various Ministers of

94

State and under them the Junior Ministers, all of whom are MPs or peers. Er . . the executive includes also government departments staffed by non-party professional civil servants . . er . . the Armed Forces, all of whom are professional of course, and the public corporations like British Rail, the Post Office and so on. Oh . . er . . perhaps I should say that ministers also have overall responsibility for affairs that are controlled by local authorities. Er . . for example, the Home Secretary is responsible for law and order in England and Wales, but local authorities for individual police forces. The Secretary of State for Education and Science decides overall education policy but local education committees deal with matters concerning the city or county. Er . . finally, we come to the judiciary . . er

. . which is . . has the function of administration of justice. Now, this is totally independent of Parliament and Government. And there are separate legal systems in England and Wales and in Scotland. Now, all these three parts are centred around this area. 'Westminster' refers to the whole of this part of London but in general parlance only to the Palace of Westminster, where the two houses of Parliament sit. Whitehall, the street to the north, is the term used to describe the activities of the executive. Downing Street, being the home of the Prime Minister, is just off Whitehall. Finally, the judiciary, which operates in all the courts of the land, has its supreme court here in the House of Lords itself. Now, if any of you have any questions, would you like . . .

(Time: 3 minutes 50 seconds)

Discussion ideas   How do the different branches of government operate in your country? How is it different from the British system? How much autonomy do the regions or states within your country have? What differences are there in, say, education systems and policies in other parts of your country?

9.9   Protest   *Picture conversation*

Student A's picture in activity 16 shows one kind of demonstration, student B's in 59 shows a different kind. Each has questions to ask the other about the relationship between the people and the government.

9.10   Freedom and the State   *Communication activity*

Student A looks at activity 17, student B at 56. Each has questions to ask the other to start off a discussion about individual freedoms, State control and protecting the public from dangers.

9.11   Guided writing   *Composition*

This is the first 200-word composition exercise. Point out the need for careful selection of points to be made and the need to express the ideas concisely.

Point out the need for students to use LINKING WORDS appropriately in their compositions. What is the effect of writing short sentences with no linking words? Or of using 'and' or 'but' all the time? Take a look at 5.4 and 8.5 again – there are more in 12.5 too. Or look at one of the passages already studied and pick out the linking words used in it.

10 Work and business

(Perhaps begin with listening exercise 10.8.)

10.1 Vocabulary

Perhaps start by making it clear that this is not a 'specialised area' of English. Advanced students should be able to tackle texts and discussions on this subject, just as an educated native speaker can. Everyone, after all, is likely to need to work for a living! (None of the reading passages are particularly 'heavy' or specialised.)

Answers

1 shareholders   2 investors   3 issuing
4 quoted Stock Exchange   5 dividends
6 research and development   7 conglomerate   8 corporation
9 subsidiaries   10 multinational   11 headquarters
12 monopoly   13 entrepreneur   14 partnership   15 manufacturing   16 shift   17 productivity   18 assembly line
19 picket line   20 shop steward   21 personnel   22 marketing
23 expenses commission   24 personal assistant   25 blue collar
white collar

Discussion ideas

If you had enough money would you invest it in shares? If you had the choice, would you become self-employed, or prefer to be an employee? Do the trade unions have too much influence these days? Give your reasons for your answers.

10.2 The telephone man   *Reading*

Answers

A 1 no response   2 'to finance public housing'   3 'we were cleared'
  4 'if that was true we wouldn't have had the anti-trust suits we had'
  5 'I worked for the stockholders. I wasn't interested in politics.'
  6 no response   7 that he leaned over backwards even to carry them
  on his shoulders – unless they were lazy or 'tried to be politicians'

B 8 as a genius   9 to increase domestic earnings   10 it was the only way they could keep Hartford Fire (Insurance company)
11 monthly week-long meetings   12 acquired subsidiaries that were too small

C He seems to like him ('affable') – but doesn't trust him completely ('persuasive talker')?

Discussion ideas   Should the management of a large (or even a small) company be tough, ruthless and repressive? Is it dog eat dog in the world of business? Which is worse: cut-throat competition between companies, or the unseemly scramble for promotion within the same company? How have management techniques changed in recent years? How do you feel about multinational companies (listen to 12.8 for more about them)?

10.3   Payment by results   _Reading_

In some occupations, workers are paid by results – and inefficient workers may be dismissed. In the USA this principle is being applied to a field of employment hitherto considered inviolable, as this article shows!
   The article is also referred to in this unit's composition exercise, 10.11.

Answers

1   sour professional relationships; encourage competition; discourage co-operation; no fair means of assessment
2   heightened public anxiety about secondary education
3   substantial incentive grants
4   to stop teachers leaving for better-paid jobs outside education
5   higher basic pay
6   probationary teachers; apprentice teachers; career teachers; then three more career rungs
7   by committees of teachers from other school districts
8   they can try out new system and return to old salary system if dissatisfied
9   on students' test results based on computer prediction
10   better to have better pay for some than no increases at all; need to get best possible deal for existing teachers
Attitude: objective, non-committal

Discussion ideas   What is your attitude to the scheme? Could it be applied in your country?

10.4 Obligation, necessity and probability

Answers

1 There's no need to make an appointment to see the personnel manager.
2 There's a (good) chance that I'll get the job I've applied for.
3 It's possible/conceivable that the economic climate will deteriorate . . .
4 It's impossible to forecast next year's turnover and profits.
5 We are obliged to repay/committed to repaying the loan.
6 In all probability/likelihood the strikers will go back to work next week.
7 It isn't necessary to have any previous experience to apply for the job.
8 I'm sure (that) there is a good explanation for all the recent absenteeism.
9 It is essential/vital to work very hard if you want to be successful . . .
10 I wouldn't be surprised if the company made a profit next year.

10.5 Word order and inversion

Answers

(Many variations are possible.) 2 did I receive/have I received 3 did they complain
4 had I when 5 had I answered/picked up than I heard/than there was 6 would/could betray/have betrayed our 7 did I talk/have I talked 8 must/should/can this be 9 could/can be understood/applied/exist 10 did he but left him too

10.6 No job to go to

This exercise concentrates on using the context to work out meaning and references. Students should underline the vocabulary items (question 1) and put a (ring) round the pronouns (question 2) in the places they occur in the passage.

Answers

1 din – noise, row suburb of a London suburb – anonymous district discards – throws away elaborate myth – complex fictional story a Standard – newspaper season ticket – monthly (or yearly) rail ticket fast-dwindling – becoming less and less dole – unemployment benefit a precarious triumph – an unsure, unsafe ascendancy simplistic attitudes – easy to understand and explain opinions camaraderie – insincere friendliness

2 line 69 – the two ex-colleagues   line 72 – the two ex-colleagues
line 76 – Dick and Jean   lines 104 and 105 – the gas and electricity
people   line 133 – the friends of the person he bought a drink
line 151 – passers-by   line 159 – the two women on the seat
line 165 – dogs   line 199 – the down and outs   line 235 – people
who stop for a chat   line 258 – their wives   line 259 – everyone
in the cinema
3 Starts the day as if going to work, catching the 8.15 train; slow walk
along the river from Waterloo Station; sits in the park; reads *The Sun*
and other papers in the public library; makes half pint last whole
lunchtime (if lucky he can get included in being bought round of drinks)
from opening time to closing time of pubs; has sandwiches on park
bench; goes to betting shop or cinema; catches train home to
unsuspecting wife

Discussion ideas   What is your reaction to the passage? Could you
ever behave like Dick? How would/do you cope
with the situation of being unemployed?

10.7 Commuting to work   *Listening*

The recorded broadcast is based on an article in *The Sunday Times* by
Caroline McGhie.

Answers

1 fresher air   less crime   better schools   proximity of countryside
2 separation from family   worry about catching trains   10 hours
per week travelling   crowded trains   having to stand on trains
rail timetables control your life   some trains cancelled
3 £33,000   £50,000
4 station   30%
5 60   three   8.15 to 9.15   25
6 £1,000   rates   living costs
7 private cars   Outer London   new towns   redeveloped older
towns

Transcript

Presenter: More and more business
people who work in London are
moving out of the city to the suburbs
and the country, where life is much
quieter and cheaper. Janet Williams
has been looking at the effect of

commuting on living patterns in the
South-East. Janet?

Janet: Yes, Brian, the whole issue was
brought home to me at a dinner party
which I went to in a very fashionable
area of London. This area is 15

minutes by train from Central London and the host was complaining that his daily commute just wasn't long enough. You see, he didn't get time to read his papers in the morning. He also said that he was beginning to feel that it would be better to move out to the country, you know, maybe to a small town like Haslemere or perhaps the old city of Winchester, maybe Oxford or even Cambridge. He thought it would be worth the up-heaval of moving and he thought this for several reasons. In his opinion there's a better education for children outside the inner city, and then of course house prices are cheaper and you get out of pollution and there isn't so much burglary out in the country. He also fancied the idea of being near the countryside at weekends and of course during the week his kids and his wife would be able to go for walks and things whenever they wanted. Now, I know it sounds very good but I have my doubts about all that. You see, I think commuting long distances must be stressful. Y . . you're jostling with people, you're standing on crowded trains, you don't get a seat, you're . . you're at the mercy of rail timetables and then there are cancella-tions and they upset you and you're worried all the time whether you'll get to the station on time and it can't be good to separate your work life from your home life by 60 miles or more. And two hours in the train every day, it can't be good for you.

Presenter: Mm, er . . you said house prices are cheaper. I mean, how much cheaper?

Janet: Oh, they're substantially cheap-er. Now, if you compare the price of a house, say, in . . er . . in Bromley with one in St Leonards on the South Coast, well, a three-bedroomed semi is two-thirds the price. You know, a four-bedroom detached house is actually only half the price of a house in Bromley. At present St Leonards is

90 minutes from London, it's a long . . it's a long way, but with electrification coming it should reduce that journey by at least 20 minutes. Now, there's another important factor which affects house prices in the commuter belt and that's closeness to the nearest station. Now, in Woking I found that houses more than 20 minutes from the station are 30% cheaper.

Presenter: Really? And how frequent do trains have to be for a town to be a suitable commuter base?

Janet: Well, first of all the service should offer a journey time of around 60 minutes. Most business people think that any longer is just too much. The key time of day to look at is 8.15 to 9.15 in the morning. There should be at least three trains into London then. Now, Winchester does have just three but, you know, in Bromley where there are two stations: they have 25 trains in that time.

Presenter: As many as that? And surely the cost of travelling such long dis-tances is very high?

Janet: Oh yes, yes, but the cost is offset by the much lower rates that local authorities outside London charge and by the lower living costs general-ly. That said, you do have to budget for at least £1,000 in fares per year and that would come very bitter, I think.

Presenter: Mm . . mm . . And so the trend is for more and more people to leave London and find homes in the country and to come in by train?

Janet: Oh no, not really. You see, there are three trends that are contradicting what I've been saying. In the first place the number of people using the railways is dropping every year, there's an increase in the use of private cars, you see. And then they're re-locating offices to Outer London, to nearer where the suburban Londoners live. You know, Croydon for example or in the north, Watford. And then there's also the relocation of offices and factories to new towns or to redeveloped older towns – the places that are further from London than it would be com .. comfortable to c .. to commute – places like Swindon, Milton Keynes, you know where you can live and work in the same town.

Presenter: Yes .. er .. and a much more pleasant prospect than facing the crowds and the tension of life in the city, I'm sure you'd agree, Janet.
Janet: Oh yes, but most Londoners don't have the choice. As a broadcaster, I feel very trapped actually.

(Time: 4 minutes 10 seconds)

<u>Discussion ideas</u>   Do the members of the class commute long distances to work, or do their parents? What's the effect of this on their lives? What is the maximum tolerable commuting time for them? Would they rather live in the country and commute into the city to work, or live in the centre, or live in the suburbs?

10.8   Women in business   *Listening*

The conversation is based on an article in *Newsweek*.

Answers

1   33%   10%   40%
2   Marisa Bellisario – Italtel – telecommunications – head
    Debbie Moore – Pineapple Dance Studios – fitness – founder
    Geneviève Gomez – Banque Indosuez – banking – secretary general
    Grete Schickedanz – Quelle – mail order – owner
3   exceptions   rule
4   husbands   families   role models   bottom
5   qualifications   opportunities   European
6   self-employed   a quarter
7   15   30s   board
8   five   level/grade   common
9   'organising'   'boss'
10 learn to think of themselves

Transcript

Tom: ... six months ago I started my new job.
Sally: Oh yes, tell me.
Tom: Well, it's very unusual actually, because I've got two bosses and they're both women.
Sally: Gosh, that is unusual. Specially in the UK. You know, according to an article I read, 10% of managerial posts in the UK are held by women, right? But they're 40% of the workforce. Now, it's very different in the USA, I mean, 33% of managers are women over there. The UK's about average for Europe .. for .. for .. Western Europe anyway.

102

Tom: Did .. did you see that programme about successful women the other
evening on telly?

Sally: Oh yes, that's right. Er .. about
the woman who founded Pineapple
Dance Studios.

Tom: That's right, Debbie Moore. I ..
she must have a marvellous business
brain to go .. to go public like .. and I
mean all that money. Um .. and there
was .. um .. er .. ooh .. er .. the
Italian .. um .. er .. Marisa Bellisario.

Sally: She's the head of that big bank in
France, isn't she?

Tom: Oh, no, no, no, no. No, that's ..
um .. Geneviève Gomez, s .. secretary
general of the Banque Indosuez. No,
no the one I'm .. mentioned is .. she's
the head of Italtel, the Italian telecommunications company, it's sort of
equivalent of British Telecom. And
then there was that marvellous German woman, do you remember, um ..
oh, I can't remember her name, Grete
something.

Sally: Oh, the queen of mail order in
Germany! Yes. Yes, she runs that mail
order house .. er .. Quelle, yes? But
you see those are just exceptions that
prove the rule: it is very hard for
women to get to the top.

Tom: Mmm .. a lot of the top female
executives apparently work in companies founded by their husbands or
.. or their families, I'm told . . .

Sally: Mmm, but you see those aren't
really suitable role models for .. for
young women in business ordinarily. I
mean, they have to start at the bottom
.. er .. they .. don't have a sort of,
you know, fast run up to the top, do
they?

Tom: Mmm, so do you think they're
discriminated against because they're
women?

Sally: No, I'm not sure about that. I
think that's probably more a thing of
the past, it's just that it is a very long
hard struggle. And you see in this day
and age young men and women enter
the job market with the same qualifications and they have the same
opportunities for the very first time in
European history.

Tom: Mmm, but salaries for women
haven't kept pace with the opportunities, have they?

Sally: No, that's true. I read that in
France, for example, women get a
third less than men. Actually, the best
way to become a boss, you see, is to
start out as one, to become self-
employed. Well, it .. it's true, i .. in
West Germany a quarter of new
businesses are started by women, a ..
and the proportion of these female
entrepreneurs are rising all the time. I
mean, y .. you can see it in sort of
enrolments at professional schools
and management colleges, it reflects it.

Tom: Mm .. you said just now that the
opportunities are equal for the first
time in .. first time in European
history?

Sally: Mmm, yes. Now .. now the
barriers have fallen, you see. I mean, I
suppose about – ooh, what – 15 years
ago women in Britain started to get
really substantial numbers of managerial posts. Well these women are now
in their – what would it be – mid-
thirties. So in ten years' time they'll be
on the board.

Tom: Oh, there's no doubt in my mind
that women can be as effective as men
in business. And I think companies are
starting to value women. A friend of
mine works for the National Westminster Bank and .. er .. women who
leave to have children .. er .. get up to
five years' leave of absence and yet
they can return to the job at exactly
the same level as before.

Sally: Yes, there .. that's very good,
there are lots of schemes like that
now. The basic problem is that
women themselves don't, well at least
many women don't accept the fact
that they are equal. They think that
men are better at organising or being
the boss. I mean, it's just, you know,
it's conditioning.

103

Tom: So the answer's education then, you think?

Sally: Yes. Yes, I think w . . women have to be taught that if they want to *be* equal, they've got to think of themselves as equal. There's . . there's no other way really.

Tom: Well, that's just what my . . one of my bosses was saying the other day . . .

(Time: 3 minutes 45 seconds)

Discussion ideas Do you agree with what Sally says? Would you prefer to have a woman or a man as a boss? Or doesn't it make any difference? How is the position of women in business in your country comparable to the position described in the conversation?

10.9   On a wing and a paper clip   *Pronunciation*

In this activity each student has a 'jigsaw' of different paragraphs of an article from *The Sunday Times*. Student A has the even-numbered paragraphs in activity 18; student B has the odd-numbered ones in 57.

Listen carefully to everyone's pronunciation and point out any improvements they should try to make. Encourage them to evaluate and discuss the techniques of management training described in the article.

10.10   Paper engineering   *Communication activity*

Working in groups, students have to solve the problem given in the Student's Book. Make sure they are conversant with the 'rules' laid down there and give out the necessary equipment (A4 paper and a paper clip to each group). With no experimental flights allowed, there should be some intense discussion about the theory and practice of constructing paper gliders.

10.11   Writing a formal letter   *Composition*

Maybe look at some published Letters to the Editor to get ideas on the formal style of language required. One partner in a pair could write a letter in favour of the scheme and the other a letter against the scheme, perhaps.

Point out the need for there to be a good balance of SHORT AND LONG SENTENCES in such a letter. What is the effect of very long sentences on a reader? What is the effect of a series of very short sentences? Is it more important to impress the reader with your education and erudition, or to make your points clearly and succinctly?

11   The future

(Perhaps begin with listening exercise 11.8.)

11.1   Vocabulary

Perhaps start by asking members of the class to predict how life will be
different in 20 years' time. What changes do they foresee in technology,
social life and in politics?

Discussion ideas   What are the changes likely in the future,
suggested in the last few questions? Are the
members of the class optimistic, pessimistic, curious or indifferent about
what the future holds in store for them? What use do they make of
computers in their studies, leisure time or work? How has their work been
transformed by the advent of computers?

11.2   Down with offices!   *Reading*

105

employees   8 traffic jams, dying railways   9 30   10 existing offices   11 15 to 20%   12 by monitoring operators' key strokes
Writer's attitude: balanced, shows both sides of the issue

Discussion ideas in Student's Book.

11.3   Gloom mongers at bay   *Reading*

Answers   2 6 to 6.5 billion   3 go down   4 couples will choose between having children or having higher living standard   5 production and yields rising   6 agricultural land area growing   7 more food and less expensive   8 food production growing faster   9 no shortage   10 demand will drop as expense rises   11 switch to alternative commodities
12 Repetition: 'Ask . . . Ask . . .Ask . . .' 'and they will say . . . and they will say' – He's setting up arguments that will be shot down later in the article
13 Rhetorical questions: 'Will we be able to feed . . .?', 'What about other commodities?' etc. – Putting questions that the sceptical reader may have in his or her mind
14 Whose opinion: the writer's (up to now he's been reporting the Henley Centre's)
15 The real problems; for *discussion*

Discussion ideas   Do you accept the Henley Centre's findings? Consider each of the points made.

11.4   Prepositions and particles   *Use of English*

(Nemesis was the ancient Greek goddess of retribution.)

Answers   1 on   2 out   3 by   4 to   5 by
6 in   7 of   8 at   9 from   10 to
11 At   12 into/through   13 with   14 of/round   15 of
16 into   17 for   18 to   19 for   20 by   21 from/of
22 in   23 for/of   24 since   25 to   26 On   27 of
28 out   29 On   30 between   31 off   32 with   33 with
34 to   35 by   36 at   37 for

11.5 Idioms with KEEP and GIVE   *Use of English*

Answers

1 Will you please keep me company for a while?
2 He's going to keep himself to himself for a time.
3 I couldn't keep a straight face when he told me of his plan.
4 The staff are going to be kept in the dark about the firm's plans . . .
5 I'll keep an open mind until we've discussed it.
6 I'll keep away from her until she's feeling more optimistic.
7 Try to keep your head even if you don't know what's going to happen.
8 In future we're not going to worry about keeping up with the Joneses.
9 Reserves of copper and other minerals will eventually give out.
10 I'll never give away the secret information.
11 She gave me to understand that she'd be leaving any day.
12 All this talk about gloom and doom gives me the creeps.

11.6 Coming soon   *Questions and summary*

Background

Sir Clive Sinclair invented the pocket calculator, was responsible for the popularity of home computers in Britain and is one of the leading lights of modern high tech industry. (His revolutionary C5 electric vehicle is described in 16.6.)

Answers

1 daunt – discourage   progenitors – creators   deem ourselves –
  consider ourselves to be   triggered – set off   founts of knowledge –
  sources of information and expertise   falling prey – becoming
  vulnerable   surrogate – substitute
2 able to design themselves and reproduce, once they surpass human
  intelligence
3 by imports and automated production (robots)
4 complete expertise of an experienced person transferred into the memory
  of a computer and able to be called upon by anyone at any time
5 computers will have more patience and knowledge – and there will be
  one 'tutor' for every child (no more jobs for teachers?)
6 medical advice and monitoring in the home; fewer jobs, more leisure,
  better education – time to appreciate art, music and science; robots to do
  the menial household tasks (*or* maybe they'll take over and live like the
  ancient Greeks, leaving us to do the menial jobs, then – if they're so
  clever??)

Which of the predictions made do you feel sceptical of? Which are you fearful of and which do you look forward to?

11.7 Journey into space   *Listening*

The information is based on an article by Ian Ridpath in *The Guardian*. Play the recording twice, but tell students to answer the questions during the *second* playing or to start *between* the two playings.

Answers

True: 2, 4, 5, 6, 10, 11, 13, 16, 18, 20
False: 1, 3, 7, 8, 9, 12, 14, 15, 17, 19

Transcript

Just imagine that you are strapped into the Space Shuttle, wearing just your light flame-proof uniform, without a space suit, just a helmet in case of leaks. You are on the mid-deck, 60 metres above the ground. Above you the astronauts are making their final flight checks. You hear three bangs as the engines ignite. It's seven seconds till lift-off. Now the main engines are igniting and the vehicle tilts and rocks. There are two very loud explosions as the boosters ignite and the Shuttle starts to rise like a high-speed lift. You see the launch tower going past and the world seems to spin as the Shuttle changes course over the deep blue Atlantic beneath the bright blue sky. You have no sensation of speed. The acceleration feels like a heavy hand pushing you back. Your arms and legs feel twice as heavy as on Earth. The acceleration stops increasing, or so it seems. You are now going faster than the speed of sound. The ride becomes quieter and smoother. The sky is now black. You see bright orange flames as the solid rockets fall away. You are still going nearly 5,000 kilometres per hour and it's only been 8½ minutes since take-off. Now you're starting to feel weightlessness, it feels almost like hanging upside down. The blood is rushing to your head; your face is going puffy; your nose is stuffed up; your legs are getting thinner; you experience slight headache and nausea. It is now 12 minutes after lift-off and the orbital manoeuvring engines put the Shuttle into orbit. You unstrap. You explore the sensation of being weightless; your hands go out to steady yourself; your knees bend and your arms float up in front of you. It takes a while to get used to it. After some experimentation you can push yourself against the walls to move in any direction up or down, though it's not clear which way is up or down anyway. You go to the hatch to watch the astronauts working or you can look through the windows to see the Earth: it's magnificently beautiful. You can make out oceans, clouds, mountain ranges, deserts – even roads and railways and the wake of the ships at sea. There's a gorgeous sunset every 90 minutes: it's like a rainbow. Soon it's time for dinner, if you feel hungry. Just inject water into the shrimp cocktail, the rice and the broccoli, put steaks into the oven. There's fruit salad in a plastic container. After eating you wash the cutlery with a damp cloth and dispose of the leftovers. When you go to the toilet the water flows down the lavatory bowl by air pressure sucking it into a fan. You wash your hands in a similar basin and you can wash your body with a damp washcloth. Finally it's time for bed, but there are no beds – you sleep zipped up in a sleeping bag attached to the wall. Sleeping in zero gravity is very comforting and relaxing. After five days it's time to go home, so you strap yourself in for re-entry. As the Shuttle re-enters the atmosphere there's an orange glow all around the outside. Gradually you feel you're being crushed; the shock of gravity after a week's weightlessness is unpleasant. The Shuttle lands much faster than a plane; eventually it stops on the runway and you walk unsteadily down the steps to a waiting bus. Are you happy to be back on the ground or longing to be in space once again?

(Time: 3 minutes 35 seconds)

Discussion ideas   Do you fancy the idea of being a passenger on the Space Shuttle? Is this a likely kind of trip in the future for anyone? How about holidays on other planets?

11.8   Ocean city   _Listening_

The information is based on an article in _The Guardian._

Answers

1 120 million   18%   380,000 sq km
2 Sony   Steel   Telegraph & Telephone   publishing
3 300 km   2 million   60 million tonnes
4 length: 5 km   distance: 20 m
   top: housing, shops, parks, airport   2nd: transport
   3rd: high tech factories   4th: telecommunications, sewers, services
5 10,000   water tank   computer   floating   afloat
   size   sea level
6 golf courses   swimming   parks   horse   + no earthquakes

Transcript

Presenter: We've all read the science fiction stories where colonies are established in space to solve the overpopulation problem on Earth. Well, a Japanese expert has now come up with a scheme that sounds very similar but which is feasible using present-day technology: a city in the middle of the ocean. Mike Hood reports.
Mike: Japan's main problem is cramming its large and ever-growing population into a very limited amount of space. Only 18% of the 380,000 square kilometres of land which make up the area of Japan can be used for living space. Over two-thirds of Japan's land area is mountainous and therefore unsuitable for housing the 120 million people which go to make up Japan's population. But now a

109

solution has been hit upon. Japan's foremost expert on new technology, Kiyohide Terai, has set up a study group with some of Japan's most prominent industrialists: the heads of world-famous companies, such as Sony, Mitsui, Nippon Steel, Nippon Telegraph & Telephone and the Asahi publishing group. Their answer is not a city in space but a vast steel metropolis built 300 kilometres off-shore in the Pacific Ocean to house up to two million people. If the initial city is a success, more identical cities will be built until Japan's overcrowding problem is solved. The cost of a single city at today's prices is estimated at £100 billion. Now, Ocean City, as the project is called, would look something like this: it would consist of four decks built on stilts. Each deck would be five kilometres square, that's just over three miles, and a 20-metre gap between each deck. Now the top deck, the deck open to the sky, would have the housing, the . . the shops, the parks and perhaps even an airport. The second deck would house the transport system and this would consist of tube trains, only robot trains, unmanned. Below that on the third deck is where the city would earn its living. This would house the industry: not factories as we know them, but the high technology . . er . . factories that Japan has become famous for – computer science, silicon chips. The bottom deck is the beating heart of the city, this is where it would be kept alive: the services, the . . er . . electrics, the gas, the sewers, telecommunications – all down at the bottom. Now, the city would be supported on 10,000 steel poles, each one of them hollow, 50 metres apart but not resting on the ocean floor but floating. Now to achieve . . haha . . a level, each pole would contain a water tank which would balance the enormous weight of the structure. And the level of water in each pole would be controlled by computer to ensure that the structure floats steadily, on an even keel, so in fact there would be no sense of being afloat. The city would not be affected by rough sea because of its enormous size and the height above sea level. Models of this city have been tested in water tanks which have simulated the worst sort of storms that the Pacific can throw at you. To build a single city would require 60 million tonnes of steel – now, to give you some idea of this, that would be two-thirds of Japan's annual output and five times the annual output of the UK. So, where would the money come from? Well, the idea is that it would be financed by an off-shore fund and offer tax benefits for the investors. It could in fact become a tax haven like the Cayman Islands and perhaps, looking further . . further ahead, could perhaps replace Hong Kong as a financial centre.

Presenter: Mmh . . yes. Sounds wonderful, Mike, but . . wh . . oh . . will people want to live there?

Mike: Well, Terai says and hopes that they will. Um . . they're trying to make it as much like the mainland as possible. It won't be like being on an ocean liner, there'll be golf courses, swimming pools, the parks . . er . . horse-riding clubs and of course it would have one distinct advantage over mainland Japan: there wouldn't be any earthquakes.

(Time: 4 minutes 35 seconds)

Discussion ideas   How would you like to live in such a city? What would the disadvantages be? What important facilities seem to have been forgotten in the plan? Do you think this is a feasible idea – could it ever be built?

11.9 Future fantasy or future fact? *Picture conversation*

Student A has a picture of a smug middle-aged computer user in activity 19, with questions to ask student B about the other picture. Student B has a picture of a retired couple playing with a pair of golfing robots in activity 54, with questions to ask student A about his or her picture. Point out that the questions should be considered as starting points – brief answers are not acceptable and they should coax each other to answer the questions at length.

11.10 Predictions *Communication activity*

Student A looks at 20, student B at 60. Each has some far-fetched and some realisable predictions about future events. They should discuss the effect on their own lives of such things coming true.

As you monitor the pairs at work (or groups of four with partners sharing the activity information) make sure they are not just reading the information aloud, but using it as the basis for a discussion.

11.11 Giving your opinions *Composition*

In case some members of the class are uninformed about science fiction, get the more knowledgeable ones to talk about the books and films they know.

Point out that an effective composition contains a variety of INTERESTING ADJECTIVES, which catch the reader's attention and imagination and help to make the points clearly. What is the effect of an essay with no adjectives or with very simple ones (like 'good' or 'large')? What is the best way to learn new adjectives? Take a look at one of the reading passages in this unit and see what descriptive adjectives are used and what is the effect created (you may find there are relatively few, but that these are still quite telling).

12 One world

(Perhaps begin with listening exercise 12.7.)

12.1 Vocabulary

Perhaps start by asking the class what their attitudes are to the problems of the developing countries. Which countries do belong to the so-called Third World? Is this a derogatory and unhelpful concept? Does everyone agree which these countries are?

Answers 1 Third World 2 aligned developing 3 North South 4 industrial/industrialised agriculture 5 peasants subsistence 6 cash 7 productively 8 plantations 9 exploited 10 raw materials 11 shanty towns 12 shacks/huts/dwellings sanitation 13 nourished starvation 14 drought famine 15 shortage surplus 16 relief agencies 17 labour taxes 18 colonialism 19 disease hunger 20 speech worship want fear 21 complacent 22 responsibility 23 guilty 24 soaring 25 insoluble

Discussion ideas (See above.) Is there any difference between a non-aligned country, a Third World country and a developing country? Are you optimistic or pessimistic about the future of the Third World?

12.2 Liberia   *Reading*

Answers 1 no longer needed slaves 2 it didn't seem worth possessing 3 the bottom has dropped out of the rubber market 4 if the USA hadn't given money 5 descendants of former slaves 6 found that only the 'Americos' have the necessary expertise 7 big business 8 under 10% 9 25% 10 iron ore 11 'fair' 12 none (?) – for discussion: students should justify their answers by referring to the article

Discussion ideas   How typical is Liberia of the Third World? How
would your country and how would Britain rate in
the 'At a glance' categories in the article? (Maybe too sensitive a question
for some students.)

12.3   Food in one place; need in another   *Reading*

This leader appeared in October 1984 after BBC TV cameras had brought
the plight of the starving population of Ethiopia to the attention of the
world. Even more severe famine hit Sudan soon after this.

Answers

True: 1, 2, 3, 4, 5, 8, 11, 12, 13
False: 6, 7, 9, 10, 14

Discussion ideas   Are the people of the countries south of the Sahara
still starving? What has been done to help them
since this article was written? What can *you* do to help people starving in a
faraway country? Why don't Western governments spend more money on
aid to such countries? Should they spend more than they do?

12.4   Reported speech   *Use of English*

Answers

1   They confirmed that food aid had not been getting through.
2   It was suggested that trucks (should) be sent there to help in the
  distribution of food supplies.
3   They accused Western governments of being too complacent and
  insular/of excessive complacency and insularity.
4   According to the report, donations were received from individuals and
  organisations.
5   It was reported that over £40 million had been received/were received
  during the previous ten days.
6   It was denied that there had been any lack of co-operation with relief
  workers on the spot.
7   The speaker insisted that a rapid increase in the birth rate had turned a
  crisis into a disaster.
8   It was hoped that an agreement would be reached quickly/soon.
9   They agreed that it was essential to take a long-term view of the situation.
10 He blamed the food shortages on the rapid growth in population.

113

12.5 Linking words and phrases *Use of English*

The answers marked * or † below are interchangeable. Other plausible answers may also be suggested by members of the class.

Answers

1 Meanwhile 2 after all 3 obviously*
4 Unfortunately 5 Alternatively 6 For this reason† 7 Clearly* 8 Undoubtedly* 9 This is why†
10 in the end

12.6 Letters to the editor *Questions and summary*

Answers

1 key issue – most important point timely and practicable – is made at just the right time and would work 'safe passage' – unobstructed rights to move across the area trek – walk a long distance leader – editorial
2 by not giving more aid; by only offering two aircraft; (by not responding to him?)
3 it won't get to the people who need it in time
4 through ERA, REST and the Wollo liberation agencies
5 pointing out the folly of setting up feeding centres
6 suggesting that the West is more sympathetic to Eritrea than to the Ethiopian government
7 from Port Sudan, down supply roads and through ERA in Eritrea
8 sending food aid to Port Sudan, Mekele and Djibouti; allowing rebel relief agencies to distribute food aid; by allowing safe passage between government-controlled areas and rebel-controlled areas for vehicles with red cross markings; by getting the British and other Western governments to send food aid immediately and assist in its distribution.

12.7 Averting calamity *Listening*

Answers

1 £1 £100 £1,000 labour-intensive capital
2 villages a short while all his life fishing tackle self-sufficient self-reliant independent £5,000
3 subsistence exploit
4 knowledge dependent slowly

5 $6 billion $8 billion   Brazil, Switzerland, Israel   arms
   health services
6 export   debts   investment

Transcript

Interviewer: According to a recent book, the West's ways of trying to help the Third World may have been totally misguided in the past; and today we've got Jane Newsome here, who's worked in West Africa and South-East Asia, and she's going to talk about the book's findings. Over to you, Jane.

Jane: Thank you. Brian May in his book *The Third World Calamity* suggests that there are six ways of averting what he maintains is certain disaster. His first point: no economic activity should be encouraged that does not contain the certain means of absorbing those it deprives of their traditional work.

Interviewer: Now, just a minute. Does .. does this mean that industrialisation is a bad thing for a developing country?

Jane: No, not necessarily. But in a modern Western-style factory each workplace costs several thousand pounds to create, such factories in Third World countries generally replace work done by traditional methods, by skilled craftsmen, and the work is done by unskilled labour. What would be better would be what E. F. Schumacher suggests: instead of £1,000 workplaces being created to replace £1 jobs, some sort of intermediate technology – £100 workplaces – should be sought. Moreover non-labour-intensive industries, such as automated production absorbs large amounts of capital and doesn't benefit the labour market in the developing country. Brian May's second point: attempted rural development should be from village level up – money should be diverted from grandiose uneconomic projects and devoted to simpler ones.

Interviewer: Well, now look, it's been said that there are in fact two million villages in the Third World but surely in actual fact it's the urban population that's rising steadily up.

Jane: Yes, that's because of drift from unproductive land to hopes of employment in cities. Now the only way to stop this is by developing the land and getting farmers to help themselves. As the saying goes: 'Give a man a fish and you're helping him a little for a very short while; teach him to fish and you'll help him all his life to help himself.'

Interviewer: That's true.

Jane: Now, better still: teach him to make his own fishing tackle, rather than supply him with fishing equipment, and he'll become not only self-sufficient but self-reliant and independent as well.

Interviewer: Well .. er .. maybe, but ah .. I mean, what kind of grandiose projects are you actually referring to?

Jane: Well, take the huge dam on the Sokoto River in Nigeria. Now that dam is longer than the Aswan Dam in Egypt and it cost 200 million. Now the main aim for this dam is to irrigate 30,000 hectares at a cost of £5,000 per hectare. Now that's typical of many such projects financed by the World Bank, constructed by Western consortiums. Brian May's third point: there should be a serious effort to prevent the slightly better off getting all the benefits in the incessant battle for a margin above subsistence.

Interviewer: Well, now look .. ah .. are you, or perhaps .. er .. Brian May trying to suggest that we have a group of corrupt officials simply trying to sell off food aid?

Jane: No. No, that's not what I mean at all. But with high unemployment and rising populations, anyone who can provide land or work for people who need to grow food or earn money to buy food is in a very advantageous position. With no social security system people are prepared to do anything in order to keep their families alive – including working for a subsistence wage. I'm not suggesting that entrepreneurs and landlords are cynically exploiting their poor workers and tenants. It's a product of the system. And to maintain their own standards of living they have to exploit other people – I'm sorry, maybe that word's a bit strong, too negative – but they do have to make their living. Brian May's fourth point: that special efforts should be made in . . in places of extreme suffering; organisations like Oxfam and Frères des Hommes are best suited to deal with these kinds of problems.

Interviewer: Why is that?

Jane: Well, they've developed expert skills at supplying and dealing with food aid and providing gifts of knowledge as well as money. It's far more valuable to teach people than to give them money and make them dependent. But for, say, famine relief, food distributed by international agencies has a better chance of reaching the needy quickly than if it's sent via governments. His fifth point: that sales of arms to Third World countries have to be drastically reduced, even though this might cause a slight reduction in living standards in the West.

Interviewer: Ah yes, now look, Jane, surely arms a . . are given to developing countries by . . by both the Western and the Eastern Bloc countries?

Jane: Yes, true. Um . . US military aid to Third World countries in 1984 was $6 billion, compared with the $8 billion in foreign aid. Soviet figures are much higher. But sales of equipment is much much higher and from most Western countries, including even Brazil, Switzerland and Israel. The point is that too high a proportion of poor countries' national budget is devoted to buying arms from the West or the East. Money that would be better spent on . . on health services, for example.

Interviewer: I see. And the . . er . . final point, Jane.

Jane: Six, yes: for any of these provisions to succeed the policy of the World Bank must be overhauled; pressures must be put on Third World countries to carry out the policies I've mentioned. Present policy seems to be to get developing countries to export more to pay their debts and adopt large-scale schemes requiring massive investment for a dubious benefit for the people. Taking advantage of cheap labour seems to be the way that the West continues to treat developing countries as present-day colonies.

Interviewer: Thank you very much.

(Time: 5 minutes 50 seconds)

Discussion ideas

Which of the points made do you agree with? How can arms sales, for example, be discouraged? Does your country 'exploit' the cheap labour, cheap food and raw materials available in poorer countries? What is your country's policy towards people from poorer countries seeking work in your country?

12.8   Multinational companies   *Listening*

Two goes at this information-packed conversation are recommended.

<u>*Answers*</u>   1 General Motors   2 BP (and also than GM
and Exxon!)   3 can be dismissed easily
4 female workers   5 Coca Cola and hamburgers   6 endangered the
lives of babies   7 contribute to Conservative Party funds   8 was of
no benefit to the people   9 the Prime Minister   10 can operate in
secrecy
11 within   12 43   13 prices   profits   high tax   low tax
exchange   tariffs   repatriate   14 corporation   import   property
excise   15 colonial   cash crops (pineapples, bananas, sugar)
soft drinks   high tar   drugs   junk   left-wing   right-wing parties
modern sector   poorer   16 lobby   bribe   alliances

Transcript

Judy: Listen, it says here that one third
of all world trade consists of multinational companies trading with themselves.
Kerry: What, with each other do you
mean?
Judy: No, no. Within their own organisations, between subsidiaries in
different countries. There's a lot more
here on the same subject, shall I tell
you?
Kerry: Mmm, go ahead.
Judy: Of the hundred largest economic
powers in the world, 57 are countries
but 43 are multinational companies.
Kerry: Wh . . you mean to say that
General Motors wields more economic power than many Third World
countries?
Judy: Both GM and Exxon are larger in
terms of world trade than Switzerland
or Saudi Arabia. And British
Petroleum is larger than Belgium,
Greece or Finland. 50% of US exports
are within multinationals. And the UK
figure is 30%.
Kerry: So the normal market mechan-
ism doesn't apply. They can actually
charge themselves what they want,

they can fix their prices to suit themselves.
Judy: Mm. Not only that but they can
make nonsense of the idea that there is
a free market because they can shift
profits from high tax countries . . .
Kerry: What, like America or . . er . .
the United Kingdom?
Judy: Yes, to low tax countries. And
they can make profits from currency
fluctuations and avoid exchange controls.
Kerry: I see, and of course that's something which smaller companies can't
do, so they're at a financial disadvan-
tage.
Judy: Absolutely. They can circumvent
tariffs and import-export restrictions.
Kerry: How? Oh, by . . by selling or
buying from subsidiaries in other
countries, I see. And of course they
can repatriate profits from other
countries to the mother country, especially profits from the developing
countries.
Judy: Mm. I mean, a typical set-up is
for a multinational company to have
its factories in free-trade zones in
South-East Asia, where of course the

117

governments are very eager to get employment for their people. So they enjoy freedom from corporation taxes, import duties, property taxes and excise duties. And of course they get monetary incentives from the government concerned.

Kerry: Right, and of course they also get political incentives like .. er .. a guarantee of no unions in certain countries and a plentiful supply of well-disciplined, cheap and disposable labour.

Judy: Oh yes! I mean, for instance, silicon chips are assembled under microscopes by semi-skilled young women in f .. the free-trade zones in Malaysia and the Philippines.

Kerry: I've heard of that. And being so powerful they can actually exercise a control – it's like a colonial power in the Third World.

Judy: Absolutely. As they can operate through subsidiaries in the countries concerned, there's no foreign influence apparent. But they can exercise a very harmful influence: I mean, substituting cash crops for self-sufficiency in food.

Kerry: Right, like .. um .. harvesting pineapples and bananas .. er .. and processing sugar for export when the people are starving for lack of food themselves.

Judy: They can edge out indigenous entrepreneurs.

Kerry: Yes, because of their ability to invest capital at will.

Judy: And alter consumption patterns harmfully.

Kerry: Right, like .. um .. encouraging sales of soft drinks and high tar cigarettes and unsafe drugs and junk foods in the poorer countries. Like Nestlés selling powdered milk in Africa, where they're directly responsible for threatening African babies' health.

Judy: They apply the ethics of the market place: give as little as possible and take as much as possible.

Kerry: Mm, without getting any bad publicity if things happen to go wrong.

Judy: Oh .. haha .. yes. They can even interfere in the political life of a country by bringing down left-wing governments or encouraging right-wing parties.

Kerry: Even in the United Kingdom where contributions from the multinationals help finance the Conservative Party.

Judy: Another effect is the creation of a small modern sector of the economy of a poor country leaving the majority of the people poorer.

Kerry: Right, just like under the Shah, this .. this is what happened in Iran. The huge steel-making industry and other projects were encouraged by the multinationals and this ate up all the revenue that they got from oil exports.

Judy: The power they can wield is what seems to affect their profits more than their efficiency or their sensitivity to customers' preferences. They have specialists who can lobby, bribe and form alliances with politicians, just so that they can increase sales or maintain their monopolies or edge out local competition.

Kerry: Mm, that reminds me of the Lockheed airplane scandal in Japan, do you remember? Where the Prime Minister took bribes so that Tristars would be bought.

Judy: It can even happen in the company's mother country. Take the way in which Chrysler persuaded President Carter to rescue them.

Kerry: Mm, and British Leyland was rescued by the United Kingdom's government.

Judy: So if they can do this in Japan, the USA and the UK, imagine what they can do in a small Third World country crying out for foreign investment and a few more jobs for its people.

Kerry: Well, the question is: how can this power be controlled?

Judy: It probably can't, because the multinationals are more powerful than their host country. And they have a more effective political set-up than a country, whose government changes periodically and is subject to public scrutiny.

Kerry: So then the 'politicians' within a multinational really can work behind closed doors!

(Time: 5 minutes)

Discussion ideas Do you agree with the opinions expressed in the conversation? What 'good deeds' are multinational companies capable of, do you think? What's the harm of selling, for example, soft drinks to people in poorer countries? Have there been any similar bribery scandals recently? What other examples of the harmful influence of multinational companies have been in the news lately?

12.9 Small is Beautiful   *Pronunciation*

Student A looks at activity 21, while B looks at 61. Each has an extract from E. F. Schumacher's *Small is Beautiful* to read, comment on and then discuss. Draw students' attention to any pronunciation errors you overhear.

12.10 National income and   *Communication activity*
population

Student A has half of two 'cartograms' showing national income and population (in activity 22). Student B has the other half of each cartogram in activity 62. They have to convey the information to each other and to discuss its implications.

12.11 Writing an analysis   *Composition*

The difficulty presented here is one of organising disparate ideas and examples into one coherent whole. Discussion and notes (arranged in a linear pattern rather than the diagrammatic pattern shown) are essential.

Point out the need for ATTITUDE WORDS to be used appropriately in such an essay. These are words like 'clearly', 'obviously', 'evidently', 'undoubtedly', 'unfortunately' and so on (see 12.5). What other similar adverbial expressions can the members of the class think of? What is the effect of using these words? What would be the effect of omitting such words from this particular essay?

(Other examples: 'It seems clear to me . . .', 'Another important point is . . .', 'It is distressing to discover that . . .', 'They should be ashamed that . . .', 'It is shocking that . . .', 'It is appalling that . . .', etc.)

13 History

(Perhaps begin with listening exercise 13.7.)

13.1 Vocabulary

Perhaps start by finding out what everybody considers to be 'history': how long ago does an event have to be to be historical? What kind of events do they consider to be historic? What does history have to teach us today? Is history fascinating, dull, irrelevant or what?

Answers

1 historic   2 historical   3 interpreting
4 architecture   5 artifacts   6 Iron Age
7 archaeologist   8 site   9 good old days   10 nostalgia
11 medieval   12 anachronism   13 Victorian   14 manuscripts
chronicles   15 posterity   16 ancestors   17 predecessor
successor   18 pre-war   19 ruins   20 prehistoric
21 themselves   22 biography   23 misfortunes   24 guide
25 learnt anything from
(Of course, 21 to 25 are the original words – other answers may be equally plausible, and should provoke some discussion.)

Discussion ideas

(See above.) What is the most significant historical event to have happened in your country during *this* century, the 19th century and during the 18th century? Why were these events so important?

13.2 Landfall on Tahiti   *Reading*

Background

Alan Moorehead, Australian-born war correspondent and writer, is well known for his well-researched and readable historical books. *The Fatal Impact* (1966) is an account of the effects of European influences on the native peoples of the Pacific and Australasia. His other books include *Gallipoli*, *The White Nile* and *The Blue Nile*.

1 no   2 none   3 scientist   4 wonder
5 no great wonder   6 ? sex, relaxation, fresh
food, R & R   7 doctors: diseases brought by the Europeans   priests:
non-adherence to alien moral codes   administrators and policemen: non-
adherence to alien code of laws   8 yes, but not at first   9 size of their
sailing ship, strange clothes, marvellous trinkets and gadgets   10 the
Tahitians – sympathy, pity   Cook – approval   the visitors who came after
Cook – antipathy, disapproval

Discussion ideas   Can 'primitive' cultures survive the influence of
'civilisation'? How could they be protected? What
might have happened if no Europeans had 'discovered' Tahiti?

13.3   JFK, the knight in not-so-shining armour   *Reading*

This article is a challenging one, containing a lot of difficult vocabulary. For
this reason, the ten multiple-choice questions should be done *before* the ten
vocabulary questions at the end, so that students can concentrate on getting
the gist of the article first of all. However, as in the exam, one or two of the
alternatives are (deliberately) debatable and you or the class may well
disagree with some of the answers suggested below!

Background   The article assumes quite a lot of knowledge of the
recent history of the USA. It may be necessary for
some members of the class to be informed or reminded about some of the
events and concepts:
Watergate (1974); the Bay of Pigs US-backed invasion of Cuba (1961); the
Cuban Missile crisis (1962) – when the world was on the brink of nuclear
war; Teddy (Edward) Kennedy's Presidential campaign (1980); Camelot,
the legendary castle of King Arthur and his court, but here the 'court' of the
Kennedys; PT 109, the patrol boat commanded by the young Jack Kennedy,
that attacked a German destroyer (in the Hollywood film starring Cliff
Robertson); Chappaquiddick (1969).

Answers

1   his youngest brother's conspicuous incompetence
2   have had their shortcomings exposed in books about them
3   the Kennedy family
4   shared their father's taste for womanising
5   friends of the Kennedy clan
6   ruined
7   did nothing outstandingly brave

8 failure
9 rash
10 is likely to change

bear-garden – unruly place   demeaning – humiliating   halo – saintly
image   went ape – went crazy   eschews – avoids   well aired –
written about at length   hyperbole – exaggeration   compliant – easily
influenced   to save face – to avoid public humiliation   to rekindle the
flame in 1980 – to reactivate public enthusiasm for the Kennedy name (in
his Presidential campaign) in 1980

Discussion ideas   Describe the public image of John F. Kennedy.
What can you say about his brothers, Robert
(Bobby) and Edward (Teddy)? Pooling everyone's knowledge, what do the
members of the class know about the achievements and careers of Franklin
D. Roosevelt, Richard M. Nixon, Jimmy Carter, Lyndon B. Johnson and
Gerald Ford? What are each of these former Presidents now chiefly
remembered for? Which recent US Presidents (including the present
incumbent) do you admire most and why? And which do you believe to be
the worst and why? Or are they all equally incompetent, ruthless and
dislikeable, perhaps? How much do our perceptions of leaders change with
hindsight? Does history show that all great men had feet of clay?

13.4 Collocations   *Use of English*

Answers   (The first given was in the original text.)
1 opportunities, homes   2 size, area
3 lead, example   4 domination, supremacy   5 race, minority
6 destruction, downfall   7 war, slaughter, conflict, *etc.*   8 visible,
stirring   9 uprising, revolution   10 retrospect   11 phase
12 imprint, stamp   13 tempo, rate, speed   14 spread
15 traditions, customs   16 process   17 ages   18 society
19 ill   20 wildfire

13.5 Idioms with BREAK, BRING   *Use of English*
and CALL

Answers

1 Negotiations between the two sides were broken off.
2 In 1945 Allied forces broke through the German defences . . .
3 Fighting broke out between Hindus and Moslems . . .

4   Bangladesh broke away from West Pakistan in 1971.
5   The Potato Famine brought about the death of a quarter of the
    population . . .
6   Germany's defeat in 1918 brought down the Kaiser.
7   . . . the monarchy was brought back under his son.
8   The more I read about history the more it brings home to me how
    relevant . . .
9   They decided to risk everything by calling their enemies' bluff.
10 The attack was called off when the winter weather became severe.
11 Only unmarried men aged 18 to 41 were called up in the First World
    War . . .
12 This calls to mind Henry Ford's remark: 'History is bunk.'

13.6 The Second World War   *Questions and summary*

Background

A. J. P. Taylor, whose entertaining and erudite books have delighted and stimulated scholars and general readers for many years, is also the author of *The Origins of the Second World War, English History 1914–1945, The First World War – an Illustrated History* and *The Hapsburg Monarchy.* He is the only person ever to have given a series of half-hour lectures direct to the TV camera without either notes or visual aids. His often controversial theories and sense of iconoclastic mischief have had a great influence on post-war historians.

Answers

1 clear cut – indisputably obvious   formal – official   decisive – most
   important   peripheral – not centrally important   run up – improvised   eclipsed – became far more important than   marginal –
   slight
2 During one month in 1914 all but one of the European Powers declared
   war on another power.
3 Wars in Abyssinia (Ethiopia) and China began earlier. Wars for Russia
   and America started later.
4 Mao Tse-tung and Chou Teh declared war on Japan (which occupied
   much of China at the time).
5 Because Germany dominated the whole of Western Europe.
6 Masses of foot soldiers were thrown against each other – just as in the
   time of Napoleon or the Romans; tanks only important towards the end.
7 Improvised battle tactics and war strategy
   Unexpectedly effective: aircraft carriers, jeeps, landing craft, anti-tank
   guns, tanks following infantry, atomic bombs

Unexpectedly ineffective: battleships, mass bombing, the RAF, tanks
going first
Fields of decisive action: Stalingrad (Eastern Front), Midway Island
(Pacific), El Alamein (North Africa), Caen (Normandy)

13.7   In the year I was born . . .   *Listening*

The recording is part of a seminar or discussion lesson on recent history.

Answers

1965 India & Pakistan; Vietnam; de Gaulle; demonstrations in Europe;
Russian space walk; American space walk; close-ups of Mars;
'Help!'; death penalty abolished; power cut; T. S. Eliot, Nat 'King'
Cole, Le Corbusier, Churchill, Schweitzer

1960 Congo; Nigerian independence; independence for French colonies;
US blockade of Cuba; Brasilia; summit meeting; Kennedy election
win; riots in Algiers; Sharpeville massacre; first Laser; first heart
pacemakers; 'Psycho'; *The Caretaker*; Boris Pasternak

(Everything else happened in 1969.)

Transcript

Lecturer: OK then, I asked you all to do
some research and to find out what
happened in the year you were born . .
er . . the ten most important events in
your opinion. Er . . Sue, you first.

Sue: Ooh. Um . . well, I found it very
difficult to restrict it just to ten . . um
. . so I've done approximately ten. Um
. . well, I was born in 1965 and in that
year the Vietnam War was . . um . .
raging . . er . . the American President,
President Johnson, had ordered
bombing of North Vietnam, which . .
er . . sort of started off demonstrations
on both sides of the Atlantic about the
escalation of the war. Er . . there was
another war in that year too, which
was between India and Pakistan . . er
. . there were lots of . . of border
clashes and in September of that year
India actually invaded West Pakistan.
Um . . in space . . er . . the Russian,
Alexei Leonov, floated for 20 minutes
in space in March and . . um . .

Edward White walked in space in
June for 21 minutes. Er . . and . . and
two Gemini spacecraft rendezvoused
in orbit. Um . . a . . and also Mariner
IV's close-up photos of Mars proved
that that planet was uninhabited. Um
. . in 1965 the Beatles were at their
peak and their film 'Help!' had just
gone on release. In . . er . . November,
on No . . um . . sorry, in November of
this year 30 million people's lights
went out in the USA and Canada in
the most enormous power cut and one
million people were stranded in eleva-
tors and subways. Um . . which . . um
. . started somebody . . um . . made
somebody say that nine months from
now a lot of kids are going to be
named Otis! Haha. Ah . . in . . in the
French presidential election General de
Gaulle beat François Mitterrand. Er . .
in Britain the death penalty was
abolished. Er . . in this year . . er . .
quite a few famous men died: er . . the

poet T. S. Eliot, the singer Nat 'King' Cole, the architect Le Corbusier, Winston Churchill and on the very day that I was born Albert Schweitzer died.

Lecturer: Ah, no connection. Haha. Well thank you, very good, Sue. Who's next? OK, Charles.

Charles: Ah yes, well, um . . I'm a bit older than most of us, I was . . er . . born in 1960. Anyway, in . . in that year . . a . . aside from my birthday the . . er . . let me see, the first thing that I've got written down is the . . um . . I couldn't find that many famous people who died in s . . 1960 that are . . Boris Pasternak, who wrote . . er . . *Dr Zhivago* . . er . . died in that year. Um . . in the same month that I was born, in April, Basilia became the new capital of Brazil replacing, if I remember, it replaced Rio de Janeiro. Um . . in South Africa there was . . er . . the Sharpeville . . um . . massacre when police opened fire on black demonstrators and they killed 67 people and . . er . . of course the world . . er . . opinion shifted dramatically against apartheid. Um . . e . . elsewhere in Africa . . er . . Nigeria became independent and most of France's colonies became . . er . . independent, the Ivory Coast . . er . . got its independence that year. Er . . the civil war in the Belgian Congo was going on and the province of Katanga seceded and the Belgian . . Belgians sent their troops in. And in Algeria the situation got worse and . . er . . the right-wing French extremists . . er . . were rioting in the capital. Er . . and there was a summit meeting between the . . the current leaders: Khrushchev, Eisenhower, Macmillan and de Gaulle but it broke up after this American spy plane was shot down, I think it was . . er . . piloted by . . er . . Gary Powers, was shot down over the Soviet Union and the summit meeting broke up. Um . . the American relations with Cuba were getting worse and the Cuban blockade started. Um . . in entertainment . . er . . *The Caretaker* by Harold Pinter was . . er . . was first performed and . . er . . Alfred Hitchcock's 'Psycho' was released in that year. Er . . the first Laser was . . was constructed in . . er . . in 1960 and the first heart pacemakers were . . were being developed back then although they weren't perfected until . . er . . much later. And of course there was the Presidential election . . er . . in the States when . . er . . Kennedy defeated Richard Nixon. Er . . that's about it.

Lecturer: Ah, lovely, thanks. Mm . . who's next then? Come on, don't be shy!

(Time: 4 minutes 25 seconds)

<u>Discussion ideas</u> Get everyone in the class to make a similar speech about the years *they* were born in. Some research is probably needed – refer them to suitable reference works.

13.8 The emigrants   *Listening*

<u>Answers</u>   1 failure of potato crop   religious persecution
         unemployment   harvest failures
2 nothing to lose   3 gold   New York   Kansas or Oklahoma

125

4 to N. America: British, Germans, Italians, Irish, Russians
to Argentina: Spaniards, Italians   to Brazil: Portuguese, Germans
to Siberia: Russians   to N. Africa: French   to Australia: British
Slaves to USA, Brazil, Caribbean   Indians to E. and S. Africa
Chinese to California and South-East Asia
5 19th century   6 33 million   7 are the descendants of immigrants
8 looking through the phone book   9 a rich mixture

Transcript

Lecturer: . . . so from this it can be seen that the huge changes in population in the 19th century affected the cultures in all parts of the world. The population of the world grew from 900 million in 1810 to 1,600 million a century later. Now, let's look at the pattern of voluntary and enforced emigration during the 19th century. There were many reasons for people leaving their homes: the failure of the potato crop in Ireland, the religious persecution in Russia mainly of the Jews, unemployment in industrial areas . . um . . harvest failures in farming areas, but they all had one thing in common: the emigrants had nothing to lose by emigrating and there was of course the . . the wonderful romantic feel of . . of emigrating to somewhere like the USA, the New World, where there was, rumour had it, cheap or even free agricultural land on offer and where a penniless immigrant could still become a . . a millionaire. And there were examples of this . . er . . Andrew Carnegie, for example. But unfortunately they were the exception, the streets were not paved with gold and the reality for most immigrants could be a place in a . . a sweat shop factory in New York, earning as little as 8 cents an hour, or even starvation on a barren piece of land in Kansas or Oklahoma.

Student: Um . . can you tell me wh . . where the biggest exodus was from and where the immigrants went to?

Lecturer: Well, they . . they came in waves . . um . . in the 19th century the largest number of emigrants came from Britain. 11 million people went out to . . er . . the USA and Canada and 2 million the other way to Australia and New Zealand. After them came the Germans: 6 million to the US and many also went to Southern Brazil . . . Following them came the Irish. As I've said, the potato harvest failed in 1847 and those that didn't starve to death emigrated. Some came to Britain of course, but 4 million of them went to the USA. Then came the Italians: 5 million Italians emigrated to the United States, many also went to Argentina and other parts of South America. Two million Russians emigrated to the US, many of them again as I've said before were Jews escaping from certain death in the pogroms, and other Russians were forced to emigrate to Siberia, many to become virtual slaves. South America . . er . . got immigrants from the Iberian Peninsula, Spain and . . er . . particularly in Brazil, the Portuguese. The French emigrated mainly to North Africa.

Student: Um . . was it only the Europeans who emigrated?

Lecturer: No, no, there was a lot of Asian emigration around this time as well. Er . . from India they moved to East Africa and South Africa, many as indentured labourers. Some Chinese emigrated to California but many more spread out to all parts of South-East Asia: er . . Siam, Java, well, Malaya. All immigration of course was not voluntary: the slave trade continued to flourish during this period and blacks from West Africa were moved to the USA and Brazil as well as the countries of the Caribbean to become the West Indians we know today.

Student: So which countries, do you think, received the greatest number of immigrants?

Lecturer: Well, the New World of .. er .. the United States took most of them. It accepted 33 million immigrants between 1821 and 1920 and in the next 20 years another 4 million came in. Australia's population grew from a tiny number, just a few thousand people, to 5 million by 1900.

Student: And what's been the effect in .. in this century of all this immi .. emigration on .. on the countries concerned?

Lecturer: Well, the 19th century saw the most radical .. er .. distribution of culture and population and the effects can still be seen today. There are for example, in areas in Argentina where Italian is still spoken and .. er .. in

Southern Brazil areas where German is spoken even though they may be second or third generation. More radically in South-East Asia there are whole countries which speak Chinese – Singapore has a Chinese majority and these are all immigrants. And South Africa has a large Indian population as well.

Student: And is there any other evidence of .. um .. now, of this early immigration in the receiving countries?

Lecturer: Ooh yes, there are .. they can be seen in their names, for example, um .. because even when people have been absorbed into the local population or intermarried, their names are still there as evidence of their origins .. er .. you see Swedish names in the mid-west of the USA .. er .. Italian names .. er .. in the American cities. Very few countries have remained immune from this influence, with the possible exception of Japan despite its relatively recently arrived immigrant population from Korea.

(Time: 5 minutes 15 seconds)

Discussion ideas
Who in the class can trace their origins back to previous generations of immigrants? Who in the class has relations who have emigrated? Would the members of the class consider emigrating themselves? Where to? Why (not)?

13.9   100 years ago   *Picture conversation*

Student A has a reproduction of 'Answering the Emigrant's Letter' by James Collinson in activity 23. Student B has a reproduction of 'Portsmouth Dockyard' by James Tissot in activity 49. They have to answer each other's questions about the pictures.

13.10 The Aztecs and the Incas

Communication activity

Student A has information about the Incas in activity 25, student B has information about the Aztecs in 63. Each becomes an 'expert' on the civilisation and tells the other about it. It may be helpful to discuss briefly with the whole class beforehand what they know about the Spanish conquest of America and about the civilisations that existed there. Perhaps look at a map too.

13.11 Writing a 200-word essay

Composition

As the Student's Book points out, a short essay needs careful attention to the SELECTION AND ORDERING of information. Although the discussion might concentrate on Napoleon, the final composition might be about another famous figure with whom students are more familiar – a national hero or heroine of their country, for example.

In marking the completed compositions, pay particular attention to relevance and sequencing of information.

14 Mind and body

(Perhaps begin with listening exercise 14.7.)

14.1 Vocabulary

Perhaps start by asking the class how they set about staying healthy and fit. What special precautions do they take against catching diseases? Are they careful about what they eat? Do they take regular exercise?

Answers

(Some of these may provoke disagreement.)
1 a consultant, a specialist, your GP
2 chubby, flabby, overweight   3 underweight, skinny, thin
4 stress, tension, worry   5 fainted, lost consciousness, passed out
6 twinge, ache, pain   7 vaccines, preventative medicine, healthy living
8 sedative, pain-killer, tranquilliser   9 lozenges, capsules, tablets
10 pull through, get better, get well   11 rash, swelling, inflammation
12 catching, contagious, infectious   13 examination, check-up, medical
14 pulled a muscle, sprained his ankle, fractured his wrist
15 alternative, complementary, fringe
Which of the alternatives above would be your first *choice?*
16 unbalanced   17 allergy   18 psychosomatic   19 anaesthetic
20 gynaecologist   21 threw up   22 transmitted   23 eradicated
24 stomach   25 arachnophobia

Discussion ideas

What are your phobias? (Acrophobia – heights; agoraphobia – open spaces; brontophobia – thunder; claustrophobia – enclosed spaces; cynophobia – dogs; murophobia – mice; nyctophobia – darkness; ophidiophobia – snakes; aerophobia – fear of flying, etc.) Is there anyone who can honestly say they are afraid of nothing?

14.2 Simple secrets   *Reading*

The writer is himself a doctor, but no longer a practising GP – otherwise he would have had to publish this article anonymously.

1 attract fewer patients   2 deceive their
patients   3 are less easily deceived   4 like
to be deceived   5 magicians' audiences   6 the Method
7 a magician's demonstration   8 mistrustful   9 letters from cured
patients   10 their own bodies cured them   11 magician
12 self-deprecatory

Discussion ideas Do you agree with the writer's views? Do you
tend to consult a doctor if you feel unwell,
or let your body cure itself? Have you ever consulted an alternative medicine
practitioner (homoeopathic doctor – see 14.7, chiropractor, osteopath,
herbalist, hypnotherapist, faith healer, etc.)? What was your experience? If
you've never consulted one, would you ever consider doing so? Why (not)?

14.3 Slow food *Reading*

This is part of a series of articles from *The Sunday Times* promoting a new
diet and fitness programme. Like any new diet, it has to be based on a
concept that sounds 'different'. This one was published soon after the
million-selling *F-Plan* diet book by Audrey Eyton (based on high-fibre
foods).

Answers

a) 2 glucose   3 insulin   4 excess glycogen   5 liver muscles
   6 surplus fat   7 level of glucose in the blood suddenly
   8 fatigue anxiety, depression and irritability   9 sweet foods
b) 1 slowly glucose   2 insulin   3 liver & muscles surplus fat
   4 glucose in the blood steady   5 hunger fatigue
c) apples√   chips√   wholegrain bread√   semolina√   pasta√
   oranges√   rice√   baked potato with butter√

Discussion ideas Do the kinds of things you eat seem to be 'slow
foods'? What do you like to eat that is clearly 'not
good for you'? To what extent do you alter your eating habits to steer
yourself towards healthy foods or away from fattening ones?

14.4 Requests and politeness *Use of English*

Answers

2 I'd rather you didn't give me an injection.

3 Do you think you could give me something to help me sleep, doctor?
4 Would it be possible to speak to someone about my problem?
5 Would you mind not smoking in the ward, please?
6 I hope you can/will be able to give this to the sister.
7 I don't seem to have brought my medical card with me.
8 You couldn't open a window (by any chance), could you?
9 I wonder if I might/could make a phone call?
10 Could you tell me what time we have to get up in the morning?

14.5   Uses of the past tense   *Use of English*

Answers
1 weren't/wasn't   2 started trying/tried
3 was/were something I could do/take
4 hadn't drunk/had   5 had stayed at home   6 didn't/wouldn't
smoke   7 went   8 stopped/gave up/quit   9 had been more
careful when   10 went to visit her/your friend/your sister

14.6   Compulsive eaters   *Questions and summary*

Answers

1 stuff herself silly – eat far too much   binge – excessive eating
   possessed by a demon – unable to control oneself   fasting – eating
   nothing   gorge – eat too much   highly charged atmosphere –
   situation where emotions and tempers are not concealed
2 compulsive eating is like an illness; compulsive eaters don't enjoy food
   in the way greedy people do
3 half the world is starving, the other half has eating disorders
4 we are born with this preference, perhaps
5 eating the wrong sorts of food makes us even more hungry
6 they were offered food to comfort them as babies
7 learn to be relaxed about food; diet of sensible whole foods; discussion;
   support; avoiding particular foods that induce a craving

Discussion ideas   What sorts of foods do you eat to excess? What
sorts of foods do you avoid eating and why?
Do you find it hard or easy to imagine what it is like to be a
'compulsive eater'? Is a 'secret drinker' motivated by similar drives?

Answers

1 early in the 19th   2 people he knew
3 see the effects   4 cure him of vomiting and diarrhoea   5 don't know if they have   6 increases   7 insoluble
8 one   9 by anyone   10 the patient as well as the illness
11 safer
12 aconite – a cold   sepia – migraine   sand – lack of confidence + fear of failure   gold – depression   petroleum + tobacco – travel sickness

Transcript

Presenter: ... previous broadcasts we've looked at other forms of alternative medicine, including chiropractic, acupuncture and herbal remedies. Today Monica Sinclair reports on homoeopathy. Now, that's a therapy with a relatively short history I believe, Monica?

Monica: Oh well, yes, that's right, Dan. It was discovered 170 years ago by a German chemist called Samuel Hahnemann. And it was by accident. He noticed a similarity between the effects of taking quinine, that's the bark of the cinchona tree, and the symptoms of malaria. He experimented on his family and friends, getting them to take doses of quinine and then 98 other substances to see what the effect of each substance was. N .. these human guinea pigs were the 'provers' of the substances. He found that if he gave tiny doses of the same substance to a patient suffering from an illness which had identical symptoms, then the illness would be cured.

Presenter: Mm. C .. could you give us an example?

Monica: Er .. yes. Well, take arsenic. Now, taking too much of this causes vomiting and diarrhoea. If a patient has an illness which has the same symptoms then a minute dose of arsenic can bring about a cure. In Hahnemann's experiments all the patients were subjected to the single blind procedure, that is they didn't know if they'd been given the medicine or an inert powder. Now, the remarkable thing is that Hahnemann made another discovery and it's hard to believe: by progressively diluting and shaking the medicine the power of its effect actually increased and this worked with insoluble substances as well as soluble ones.

Presenter: Um .. er .. h .. how do you mean?

Monica: Well, by adding one drop of a substance, which he called the 'mother tincture', to 100 drops of liquid, then shaking it well and adding one drop of this to 100 drops of more liquid and so on he could increase the effect of the medicine even though the original tincture was no longer detectable. Modern homoeopathic remedies commonly use 30 C potency substances (i.e. a dilution of $\frac{1}{10^{60}}$ – that's ten with 60 noughts). And an insoluble substance like gold or .. or sand could be used in the same way by the same method of adding to liquid and shaking and making a new solution, the former to .. to treat depression and the latter to treat lack of confidence or fear of failure. In other words this potentisation of a substance is what gave it its power of curing. Somehow the .. the medicine acts as a catalyst to the body's immune system.

Presenter: I see. Y .. you mean rather like a vaccination?

Monica: Yes, yes. Except for the principle of potency, which immunisation doesn't use. It seems to me that the methods of homoeopathy would have been considered as far-fetched if they hadn't been successful – this is what validates them.

Presenter: Mm. Who uses homoeopathic methods in medicine today?

Monica: Well, there are two classes of practitioners: the medically unqualified quacks and qualified doctors who use the same methods. With homoeopathy the quack may be just as effective and safe as the doctor. Indeed self-medication is very effective too. The important thing is treating the illness and the patient too. The treatment must suit the temperament of the patient as well as his symptoms.

Presenter: Yes, well you .. you've told us about homoeopathy, Monica, but now can you .. er .. tell us some of its advantages over conventional medicine?

Monica: Yes. Well, the first thing is that it does work, there are numerous well-documented studies of it. Um .. the second most important thing is that there are no side-effects, unlike orthodox drugs like tranquillisers, aspirins, even coffee. Um .. and thirdly anyone can use it, anyone, by careful study of their symptoms and knowledge of the patient's personality. A mother can treat her children just as effectively as a doctor for minor ailments.

Presenter: Mm. Would you consult a homoeopathic doctor yourself?

Monica: Ooh yes. For instance, I suffer from travel sickness in cars, planes and by sea. Now, drugs from the chemist make you drowsy, they often don't even work, and a homoeopathic doctor recommended that I tried either tobacco or petroleum. Haha, amazing. Well, I tried both and the first suits my temperament best and I don't suffer from it any more. I .. I just take my tobacco tablets and I feel wonderful.

Presenter: Tablets!

Monica: Haha. Yes, and they're very cheap from the chemist's or from a health shop. You get a 30 C dose in tablet form, which you swallow or dissolve on the tongue, they're very tiny. Now, I also get migraine – or used to – and .. er .. the doctor recommended sepia, which is derived from the cuttlefish, and this works for me because I tend to have sudden changes of mood and get irritated easily.

Presenter: I see. Well, if I told you that I thought I'd got a cold coming on, could you tell me how to treat it?

Monica: Yes, aconite is good for that, but there are other remedies i .. w .. it depends how you personally react to having a cold.

Presenter: OK. Monica Sinclair, thanks very much.

Monica: Thank you.

Presenter: Next week we'll be reporting on hypnosis as another form of alternative medicine. So from me, Dan Green, goodbye.

(Time: 5 minutes 40 seconds)

Discussion ideas (See 14.2 above.) Is the speaker gullible, like the magician's audience? Can you believe in homoeopathy? What more do you know about it than was mentioned in the recording?

14.8   Was Freud a fraud?   *Listening*

The information and ideas are loosely based on an article by Prof. Hans Eysenck in *The Mail on Sunday*.

Answers

True: 2, 3, 8, 10, 11, 12, 13, 16, 17, 18, 19
False: 1, 4, 5, 6, 7, 9, 14, 15, 20
Attitude: vehement, sarcastic, scathing (?)
Impression: brusque, urbane, malicious, energetic, erudite, quick-witted, etc.

Transcript

Presenter: In most people's estimation the Viennese psycho-analyst Sigmund Freud ranks with Copernicus, Galileo, Darwin and Einstein as one of the greatest scientists of all time, in fact a true genius. Well, how true is this? Professor Carl Abrahams says we've all been fooled too long. Is that right, Professor Abrahams?

Abrahams: Yes, the truth is that Freud is one of the most successful charlatans who ever lived. He pulled the wool over his contemporaries' eyes and his followers continue to pull the wool over people's eyes today. Now, just for a start: there's no evidence whatsoever that psycho-analysis has ever cured anyone of anything. Ha .. it's become clear that Freudian psycho-analysis is pure hokum according to over 500 empirical studies of patients. Now, those who supposedly benefited from psychiatrists' treatment fared no better than those who were left to their own devices, indeed there's good evidence that it made some patients worse. Now, most professional psychiatrists know this very well, but the world is full of amateur psychiatrists like teachers, social workers, probation officers, and even parents, who attempt to apply misunderstood and speculative Freudian ideas.

Presenter: Speculative?
Abrahams: Yes, yes. Freud's so-called apparatus for explaining human behaviour is pure speculation. Also there .. there's no concrete evidence that his methods even worked for him. For example, the so-called 'wolf-man', this man who had dreams of wolves sitting in a tree outside of his house: now, he had exactly the same symptoms and the same problems for the rest of his life after supposedly being cured by Freud successfully. Freud concocted a beautifully literary story but he omitted certain factual details and he actually added his own imaginative content. Now, this has been proved by detective work in other patients he treated. Very often he clearly made an erroneous diagnosis and his treatment was unsuccessful but he chose to ignore these cases. In other words, Freud appears to have been a brilliant novelist but a lousy doctor.

Presenter: Now, Carl Jung's main criticism of Freud's work was that he placed excessive emphasis on sexuality and on childhood experiences as being the origins of neurotic disorders, wasn't it?
Abrahams: Absolutely, his equation of pleasure with sexuality was unjustified. Now, it's caught the public's imagina-

tion and kept it for the whole of this century. Take the Freudian slip that people refer to when they make a slip of the tongue .. er .. for instance: 'the breast thing to do' instead of 'the best thing to do', you see. Now this is popularly supposed to be due to a man's desire to return to his mother's body, like Oedipus, but it's .. ha .. it's all absolute rubbish of course.

Presenter: But how did Freud manage to fool people in the way you say he did?

Abrahams: Ah well, it's very interesting. Firstly he consciously set out to create a myth of himself as the misunderstood and persecuted hero, whose books were disregarded and poorly reviewed. Well, nothing could be further from the truth. Now, just look at the medical journals of the time and you will find long and enthusiastic reviews of every one of his publications. Some were even commenting back then on his genius. Indeed, the greatest myth of all is that Freud was a genius, that .. that his was a truly original mind at work. He is popularly supposed to have invented the unconscious. Well .. ha .. again this is utter nonsense. People had been writing about the unconscious mind for 2,000 years before Freud, indeed it was being widely discussed by educated people long before Freud claimed it for his own.

For example, his so-called Freudian symbolism was common knowledge in Greek and Roman times and his supposedly new method of free association had been publicised by Sir Francis Galton years before Freud claims to have invented it. Now, other theories he claimed as original had been proposed by .. er .. Pierre Janet, for instance, and so on and so on.

Presenter: Well, all right, so Freud may have been a fraud, but how has his influence been harmful?

Abrahams: Well .. er .. three instances. Number one: by encouraging speculation instead of experimental studies. Er .. number two: by encouraging .. er .. nebulous philosophising and so on. And number three: by discouraging rigorous clinical trials. Now, although Freud is not taken seriously by any self-respecting professional any more, the psycho-analysts of the world are making a very good living from the gullibility of .. er .. the public, who still believe that Freud can not only explain their problems but even that he .. that he knows how to cure them. In short, it'll be a long time before the myths, the utter myths, that Freud himself so .. so artfully created can be finally expunged.

Presenter: Professor Abrahams, thank you.

Abrahams: You're welcome.

(Time: 4 minutes 40 seconds)

Discussion ideas

To what extent are you convinced by Prof. Abrahams' diatribe? How can a psychiatrist help someone with a neurotic problem? What is the difference between a psychiatrist and a psychologist?

14.9 'Deafness risk' *Pronunciation*

This 'jigsaw' activity is based on a newspaper article about the dangers of using a Walkman personal stereo. Student A looks at activity 27, B at 65 and C at 78 – each has different paragraphs of the article.

Go round the class, drawing attention to any pronunciation errors you hear. Perhaps get some members of the class to read a paragraph each, whilst the others listen and make helpful comments. Encourage them to discuss the content of the article when they have finished reading it.

14.10 Salt *Communication activity*

In groups of three, looking at activities 29, 64 or 75, students have separate parts of a chart showing how much salt there is in different foods. They have to exchange this information and discuss it.

14.11 Writing a well-balanced essay *Composition*

The main difficulty with this composition may be in making it interesting for the reader, more than a list of advice and comments. Some attitude that predominates throughout (like Prof. Abrahams' attitude in 14.8) may help to give a feeling of completeness to the essay. Also personal examples will help.

Point out that an essay of this kind must show complete RELEVANCE TO THE QUESTION asked. Any examples that are given must be related to the points that are made. Any mention of, say, how annoying cigarette smoke is or the social effects of alcohol dependency may not be relevant in this case. Can most things be made to seem relevant if a logical connection to the topic is made explicitly?

15 War and peace

(Perhaps begin with listening exercise 15.7.)

15.1 Vocabulary

Perhaps begin by finding out who in the class likes films or books about war. Is war an inescapable part of human life? Or will the human race one day be able to end all war?

The second part of the exercise may seem off-putting to some students, with its military ranks and technical terms. Possibly, you might reassure them that even you are a little unsure about some of these! They are all, however, terms that are frequently encountered in news reports, films and fiction.

Answers

1 civil guerrilla   2 commandos/marines/rangers/troops   3 reinforcements   4 troops ammunition supplies   5 ceasefire treaty armistice   6 losses surrender   7 conscripts reservists   8 manoeuvres allies 9 horrifying/ghastly/frightful, *etc.*   10 mercenary civilian pacifist 11 balance of power   12 Intercontinental Ballistic Missiles 13 Strategic Arms Limitation Talks   14 Campaign Disarmament unilateral disarmament   15 holocaust 16 major, captain, colonel   17 admiral, lieutenant, commander 18 squadron leader, wing commander   19 petty officer, corporal, warrant officer   20 seaman, private, aircraftman   21 submarine, destroyer, aircraft carrier, cruiser   22 tank, armoured car   23 *all five*   24 barracks, parade ground, guard house   25 2: brigade 3: battalion   4: company   5: platoon

Discussion ideas   Are conventional warfare and nuclear warfare totally different concepts? Is nuclear warfare something so horrifying that it is a taboo subject (like death or cancer)? Should your country have nuclear weapons on its territory? Do young men in your country have to do military service? Does it do them any good (or harm)?

137

15.2 The end of the war

Reading

Background

Robert Graves (1895–1985) served in the First World War as an officer.
Goodbye to All That (1929) is an autobiography describing his war experiences and his relationship with other young officers (he was 19 when the war began), many of whom died in the fighting. His prose works include *I, Claudius* and *The Greek Myths* and his poems are to be found in any anthology of modern poetry.

Answers

1 really did exist   2 did not realise she was very ill   3 four   4 training soldiers who wanted to be officers   5 was overwhelmed with grief   6 detached (*though all the more moving as a result*)

Discussion ideas

What is your reaction to the passage? Why is it moving?

15.3 Three poems about war

Reading

Background

Rupert Brooke (1887–1915) became an officer on the outbreak of the war. He did not see active service, but died of an illness on his way to the Turkish front. His best-known poems are patriotic.

Wilfred Owen (1893–1918) served for three years in Flanders as an officer. His poems on the futility and horror of modern warfare were collected and published after his death by Siegfried Sassoon. He was killed by machine-gun fire on November 8th 1918, a few days before the Armistice.

Siegfried Sassoon (1886–1967) served as an officer in Flanders through-out the war. He survived the war and his poems include many written during the Second World War too. His best-known prose work is *Memoirs of a Fox-hunting Man* (1929). His poems are not all as accessible as this one.

Answers

(Some of these may be debatable.) 1 England's scenery and people   2 in spring or summer   3 his Englishness is immortal   4 the poem would still mean the same??   5 optimistic   6 has only just died   7 a man should grow up to die in this way   8 sardonic   9 incompetent   10 two typical private soldiers   11 liked him   12 sarcastic/serious?

138

Discussion ideas Which of the poems has the greatest impact for you? Consider the rhythm of each of the poems – what effects are created by these different rhythms?

15.4 Gap-filling *Use of English*

All kinds of words are missing: nouns, adjectives, prepositions, verbs, etc.

Answers

1 have   2 reason   3 any   4 emerged
5 between   6 might/could   7 explanation
8 debt   9 whether   10 concern/disquiet   11 trace/find
12 Once/Whenever   13 including/besides   14 limits   15 devote/
assign/commit   16 insignificant   17 turnover   18 long-term/
reported   19 equivalent/comparative   20 short

15.5 Idioms with MAKE *Use of English*

Answers

1 The Austrians made peace with Napoleon in 1809.
2 They couldn't make out what the enemy were trying to say.
3 The sergeant made out that three men had deserted.
4 The Russians made a stand against Napoleon's attack . . .
5 The onset of winter made things worse for the troops.
6 Seeing the enemy's guns facing him made his hair stand on end.
7 While they were on leave the sailors made the most of their freedom.
8 The guards made a good showing in the parade.
9 The indiscriminate killing of civilians makes a mockery of the treaty.
10 I make no secret of my loathing for war.

15.6 Star Wars *Questions and summary*

Answers

1 euphemisms – less direct terms for unpleasant things   counter
   measures – attack   retaliatory force – a force that could strike back
   non-military spin-offs – by-products that could be useful to civilians
   counter measures – development of weapons in response   stems
   from – is due to   abrogate – end the effect of   superseded –
   replaced

2 genuine desire to introduce effective defence system; influence of arms manufacturers, scientists and military
3 originally as means of defending population, now as means of defending military sites (ie missiles and control centres)
4 seen as offensive
5 US desire to be predominant; Soviet fear of being invaded; pressure of military, industry and scientists on politicians
6 too much money for no clearly worthwhile purpose – would only be partially effective; as a threat to the USSR it destabilises the 'balance of terror'; detracts attention from the need to freeze and abolish nuclear arms – creates a false hope which is dangerous

Discussion ideas   What is your opinion of the views expressed in the letter? Think of some more examples of euphemisms – for 'dying', for example.

15.7   The invasion of Grenada   *Listening*

US forces invaded Grenada in 1983.

Answers 1 transport planes   2 5 am   Marines
3 heavy resistance   4 7.15 am   5 8.50 am
True Blue   6 7.30 pm   Governor's   7 students   evacuated
Barbados   8 4 pm   helicopter   9 6,000   11 60   7
10 an independent state   11 nutmeg   12 a week after/soon after the coup   13 is virtually part of the USA

Transcript

Newsreader: Here is the 6 o'clock news for today, Thursday October 27. The main news: US forces which landed on Tuesday on the Caribbean island of Grenada still appear to be meeting some resistance from local and Cuban forces on the island. This report from our correspondent in Grenada, Roger Horn.

Horn: Reporters here in St George's, the tiny capital town of Grenada, are still trying to piece together the facts about what has been happening since the first American troops landed two days ago. US military sources are playing their cards close to their chests at the moment and those news confer-

ences that have taken place have been more notable for what they concealed than for what they revealed. This much is clear, however: the whole operation was launched last week when a task force of a dozen US warships, including the aircraft carrier 'Independence' and the helicopter carrier 'Guam' were diverted from their course to Lebanon towards the Caribbean. The first wave of the invasion began before dawn on Tuesday, when transport planes left Barbados, about 150 miles away, with US Rangers who were to land at Point Salines in the far west of the island. At 5 am the same day, about 400 Marines from the 'USS

140

Guam' landed at Pearls Airport on the east coast and secured it within two hours. The 'Guam' then moved to the west coast. Meanwhile the Rangers who had landed at Point Salines met heavy resistance but by 7.15 am they had secured the Cuban-built airstrip there. Their next move was to secure the True Blue medical school near the airfield, which they were able to do at 8.50 am. The same evening at 7.30, 250 Marines with five tanks and 13 amphibious vehicles landed at Grand Mal, just north of here, where they secured the British Governor's house as well as the prison at Richmond Hill and Fort Frederick. Yesterday at 9.15 am the first students from True Blue were evacuated from Point Salines airfield and a shuttle service began, ferrying troops, equipment and munitions from Barbados to Grenada. Later the same day, at 4 pm the medical students in the Grand Anse campus of the medical school were evacuated after a helicopter assault.

By now, Thursday teatime, there are 5,000 American paratroops on the island, 500 Marines and 500 Rangers. There has been continued resistance from Grenadian forces and Cubans, and US fighter planes have been making low-level attacks on Cuban posi-

tions to the south of here. So far US sources have refused to give any estimates of numbers of casualties on either side, though unofficial reports put the number of US dead at 11, at least 60 wounded (some seriously) and seven still missing. The decision to mount the invasion of this former British colony, with a population of 100,000 and whose main claim to fame so far has been its position as the world's leading exporter of nutmeg, appears to have been made very hastily by the US government.

After the coup reported on 13 October, the left-wing Prime Minister, Maurice Bishop, was arrested and on 19 October he was executed together with several members of his government by officers supporting General Hudson Austin who declared himself the new leader of Grenada, apparently with Cuban support. These events led the US to divert warships and later mount the invasion. Evidently, the US government sees its role as invader more as a stabilising influence on the Caribbean, still regarded by the President as an American lake. This is Roger Horn in St George's, Grenada. *Newsreader:* And now the rest of the news: In the Lebanon today, forces loyal to . . .

(Time: 3 minutes 50 seconds)

Discussion ideas   Was the USA justified in its action (supported by other Caribbean countries)? Is there a difference between Soviet (or Cuban or Marxist) influence in Third World countries and American (or European or capitalist) influence? Is a 'small war' like this one amusing or horrifying?

15.8 The longer Long March   *Listening*

It may be necessary to point out that the speaker uses the British pronunciation of the names – a Portuguese speaker may find this confusing! The information is based on an article by Richard Bourne in *The Guardian*.

141

Answers

1 all three reasons   2 800   3 to keep him away from Rio   4 January 1925   5 both São Paulo and Rio Grande do Sul   6 make it possible for others to overthrow the government   7 Prestes did not intend to attack Rio   8 1927   9 1,500   10 knew nothing about it   11 was an important chapter   12 rejected capitalism

Transcript

Presenter: When we hear about 'The Long March' we automatically think of Mao Tse Tung's epic journey with 100,000 men and their dependants over a distance of 12,000 kilometres, only 30,000 of whom survived. But Eileen has been looking at a longer march of smaller but no less epic qualities. Eileen?

Eileen: Yes, indeed, Tony. If you mention the Long March in Brazil people will think of an altogether different march, that of the Prestes Column in the 1920s. Let me set the scene for you. Early in the 1920s young officers in the Brazilian army were restless: their pay was poor, they had out of date equipment and were insulted by the politicians. In July 1922 the military school and the fort of Copacabana in Rio rose in revolt and when finally 18 men came out of the besieged fort they were shot by the 3,000 troops sent to attack. The 800 surviving cadets were all expelled. One officer among the survivors was a young captain of engineers, Luis Carlos Prestes; he had been ill with typhus and he hadn't taken part in the revolt. But he was under suspicion and was sent to the far south, Rio Grande do Sul, to build railways. Now, in July 1924 there was another revolt of young officers, this time in São Paulo. They held the city for 20 days before being forced to retreat to Paraguay in the west. Prestes organised a force of 1,500 poorly armed men to support them in October 1924, but was unable to break through to them until January. They were bottled up by a government force of 14,000 men under the French general Gamelin, who was French commander when Germany invaded France in 1940. Prestes and his men got to the São Paulo survivors just in time and with them formed a column of 1,500 men under Prestes as chief of staff and with Miguel Costa as commander. They slipped briefly into Paraguay and then headed into the interior of Brazil to begin their long march. Their aim was to keep government forces busy and divert them from Rio, where other young officers might have a better chance of a successful uprising. The government was naturally very worried and at one stage they mobilised 20,000 troops, the state police and even local bandits to stop the Prestes Column from getting to Rio. Even though at the time they were far away in the north-east. Eventually after 20 months and after covering 17,500 kilometres mostly on foot Prestes called a halt and with no hope of an amnesty made a fighting retreat to Bolivia. He was able to get jobs for his 400 surviving men with an English company there. It was only then that the Brazilian public first heard about Prestes. At the time of the march the state of emergency and strict censorship had kept the progress of the Column secret. A journalist from one of Brazil's leading newspapers interviewed Prestes for the first time.

Presenter: And what were the effects of the Column's march?

Eileen: Well, firstly, it paved the way for a successful revolution in 1930,

142

under Getulio Vargas. Secondly, it made the young officers heroes, they became participants in every government then until the 1960s. And, thirdly, seeing the deep contrasts in his country pointed Prestes himself towards the Communist Party, which he joined in 1934. He became its general secretary and continued as a political activist until the 1980s, with periods underground and in prison.

Presenter: Mm, he sounds a remarkable man. Thank you, Eileen.

(Time: 4 minutes 5 seconds)

Discussion ideas   What's the difference between a freedom fighter, a guerilla and a terrorist? Under what circumstances is an armed revolt against a government justifiable? Has your country ever been involved in a civil war? Describe the circumstances.

15.9   Attitudes to defence   *Picture conversation*

Student A has a picture in activity 28 of people protesting against nuclear weapons; student B has a picture in 66 of a submarine. Each has questions to ask the other about the implications of each picture.

15.10   Military spending   *Communication activity*

Each student has half of a cartogram showing the amount of money spent by different countries on their armed forces in activities 30 and 67. There is also some extra information to stimulate discussion.

15.11   Writing a 350-word composition   *Composition*

As suggested in the Student's Book, students may need to do some reading or research to prepare for this composition topic. Certainly, discussion in class is indispensable.

Point out the need for a composition to have a comprehensible OVERALL STRUCTURE. The reader must be able to see what the purpose of an essay is and how it is constructed. This involves paying attention to the introduction and conclusion; to the use of paragraphs; to a clearly expressed 'line' or attitude when giving opinions. What other elements may be important to give an essay its structure?

16   Science and technology

(Perhaps start with listening exercise 16.7 as a relatively non-technical lead-in to the topic.)

16.1   Vocabulary

Perhaps begin by discussing the role of science or technology in the lives of the members of the class. What are the five most significant or useful inventions available in the modern world – the motor car, the typewriter, the computer, the tin opener, the television, the digital clock, or what?

In this vocabulary exercise, as in the exam, students need to pay attention to structural or syntactical clues, as well as semantic ones.

Answers
1 application   2 meteorology   3 zoology
4 anthropology   5 trial and error
6 generation   7 PhD   8 controlled   9 inspiration
10 setting up   11 been raised   12 impractical   13 equipment
14 patent   15 think up   16 compound   17 catalyst
18 socket   19 fuse   20 microchip   21 knob   22 gauge
23 chassis   24 engineer   25 hand it to him

Discussion ideas   How are scientists and inventors regarded in your country – as boffins in ivory towers, or as respected pace-setters? What well-known discoveries and inventions have originated in your country?

16.2   The paper clip's grip on history   *Reading*

Answers   1 handkerchief – King Richard II   super-market trolley – Sylvan N. Goodman and a Swiss gentleman   folding pushchair – another man who died recently bifocal spectacles and rocking chair – Benjamin Franklin   television – Joseph Stalin   milk carton and paper clip – Victor Farris   scissors – Leonardo da Vinci   airport luggage trolley – Sylvan N. Goodman
2 Kennedy   3 Chernenko   4 two   5 untrue ads in press and hiring pretend shoppers   6 child can't see its parent and is vibrated

7 comfortable, good visibility, child can see its parent at work
8 five: folding bit for child or bag; stacking; won't tip up; kangaroo trick
embarrasses companions; stability and smooth running   9 look
ridiculous and harder to pedal   10 add engine at front; add big wheels
and canopy

Discussion ideas in Student's Book.

16.3   Diesel 46009 proves a point   *Reading*

Answers   1 to give the effect of a timetable   2 this is
how railway staff refer to trains   3 a loco-
motive was destroyed   4 he wanted pressmen to see he was happy
5 99.71 p.s.i.   6 away from Nottingham   7 to conform with
international regulations   8 Sir Walter's statement   9 irrelevant but
amusing   10 sceptical of   11 Ross, Dill and Northmore
12 Ross and Horrobin   13 Simmons   14 Simmons   15 Dill
and Simmons

Discussion ideas   Nuclear power stations – for and against. Do you
believe official reassurances about leaks, dangers
and justifiable expenditure?

16.4   The passive and question tags   *Use of English*

Answers

2   Television couldn't have been invented by Marconi, could it?
3   All our housework could one day be done by robots, couldn't it? (*or*
   might)
4   Professor Jones is being/going to be awarded an honorary doctorate,
   isn't he?
5   Government grants to postgraduate research students are going to be
   cut, aren't they?
6   Some amazing experiments have been carried out by research biologists
   recently, haven't they?
7   A breakthrough in electric vehicle design was not achieved until the
   mid-80s, was it?
8   No universally acceptable substitute for the petrol engine has yet been
   found, has it?
9   New uses for computers are being found all the time, aren't they?
10   A 3-D TV will have been patented by the end of the century, won't it?

16.5 Aspects of the future *Use of English*

Answers 1 to be discovered/announced   2 of doctors finding a cure for   3 will have been converted to nuclear energy/solar energy   4 will be operated   5 if everyone/ every home had   6 to having a ride/drive/go   7 won't/couldn't be a/any   8 am/get (very)   will (probably) still be used for   9 to get/have *or* until I get/can afford   10 will never be/may one day be

---

16.6 The Sinclair C5 *Questions and summary*

Background Sir Clive Sinclair (known as 'Uncle Clive' to his acolytes – you read about his visions of the future in 11.6) is the best-known name among the high-tech entrepreneurs of Britain in the eighties. He invented the pocket calculator and his best-selling ZX and Spectrum home computers brought computer games into millions of British homes and made him a multi-millionaire. The doomed C5 electric tricycle received a bad press at its launch in 1985 on the grounds that it was unsafe and looked very silly. It never took off commercially, sold only a few thousand and soon went out of production. By Christmas, remaining stocks were being sold off for £139.95. His computer company, too, was in some pretty serious financial difficulties.

The passage is an extract from a magazine advertisement. The ASA (see 7.6) subsequently upheld several complaints about this advertisement, as this article explains:

Sinclair C5 advertising criticised

By David Simpson,
Business Correspondent

Sir Clive Sinclair's electrical tricycle invention, the C5, has been dealt a further blow through a decision by the Advertising Standards Authority to uphold four out of five complaints made against the marketing campaign for the three-wheeler.

The ASA decision comes hard on the heels of Monday's revelation by Sir Clive's private company, Sinclair Vehicles, that it is to cut production of the C5 at Hoover's Merthyr Tydfil factory from 1,000 to 100 tricycles a week.

According to today's issue of the Engineer magazine, the ASA ruled that claims made in a series of advertisements for the C5 were in one instance "exaggerated" and in another "were unproven, and unjustified."

Most damagingly, the ASA has ordered Sinclair Vehicles not to repeat its claim that the C5 is "far safer than anything on two wheels," on the grounds that no evidence has been produced to support this claim.

It has also told Sinclair Vehicles to withdraw its statement that the C5, with its maximum speed of 15 mph, cruises at twice the speed of a bicycle.

Other complaints which the ASA has upheld are that Sinclair Vehicles exaggerated the aerodynamic benefits of the C5's design, and that advertisements offering the tricycle at a basic price of £399 featured photographs of a C5 equipped with optional extras.

Some 5,000 C5s were sold through a mail order campaign during January and February after its launch at the beginning of the year. Direct retail sales have proved far less successful.

About 3,000 are believed to be awaiting sale.

Answers

1 a designer's dream – an unachieved ideal   deployed – used
  endless – unceasing   the state of the art – the most modern technology
  gradient – slope   sheer fun – great enjoyment
2 a) the battery   b) steel   c) the C5   d) the body design
  e) the C5   f) the drive button   g) the feeling   h) the C5
3 polypropylene (plastic) moulded body; tyres (?)
4 20 miles at up to 15 mph
5 steering bars low down
6 licence, tax, insurance and helmet
7 OK: no licence needed, not too fast
  Not OK: may need to pedal, open top, vulnerable in traffic
8 OK: fun, open top
  Not OK: vulnerable in traffic, not fast, motorbike or small car look less silly

Discussion ideas   Like to try a C5? Ever seen one on the road?
Could electric vehicles one day replace petrol or diesel vehicles? What are the disadvantages of electric vehicles at present?

16.7 Modern airports   *Listening*

There are two parts to the recording: the whole thing can be played without interruption, or with a pause in the place indicated in the transcript. The second part may need to be played twice, but the first should not.

Answers

A Congestion; inconvenience of bussing passengers to remote aircraft stands
B 1 Gatwick (in the future)   2 de Gaulle 2   3 de Gaulle 1
   4 Frankfurt   5 Riyadh   6 Atlanta   7 Washington

C Atlanta – 11 km – limousine   Gatwick – 45 km – 30 mins by
rail   Paris – 25 km – coach *or* bus and train   Riyadh – 2 km –
taxi   Washington – 45 km – coach
D Best-liked: ? Frankfurt   Disliked: Charles de Gaulle 2

Transcript

Presenter: Modern aircraft technology is becoming more and more sophisticated with computer control of navigation, not to mention take-off and landing, as well as the development of all-weather systems for planes to be able to land and take off in almost zero visibility. We tend to lose sight of the part of air travel that can take as much of travellers' time as they spend in the air: using airports. Airport design has itself been undergoing something of a revolution, as Mark Gibson reports. Mark?

Mark: Yes, thank you, Maxine. Well, the conventional old-fashioned airport consists of a central terminal with aircraft parked all around it, some close enough for passengers to use the power-operated gangways joined to the terminal building, and others further away and accessible only by bus. Indeed most modern airports are like this all over the world, with the arrival and departure areas conventionally separated on different floors of the terminal. But airports all have two big problems. Now the first, and you can go to Heathrow on a busy summer weekend and see what I mean, is the congestion within the terminal and this can't be solved by just building bigger and bigger terminals. The second is the inconvenience of bussing passengers for certain flights to remote stands on the other side of the airfield. Now, one way of solving these problems is to have two terminals: one for the time-consuming procedures involved in international flights and the other for the faster turnround of domestic flights. But a busy airport of course

may need more than two.

Presenter: Now, you've been looking at six different airports, haven't you?

Mark: Yes I have. Er . . and the first I'm going to look at, the closest to home, is Gatwick. Now, most flights from there are international and its design ideas for the future are to build up to four remote satellites at some distance from the central terminal building . . er . . access to these would be by driverless railcars. Now these satellites would contain all the facilities of the central terminal: shops, banks, bars, restaurants, etc. Gatwick Two is the first stage of this, it . . it's wonderfully designed, it's functional, yet still as we say 'user-friendly'. Now, a variation on the idea of having remote concourses can be seen at Hartsfield Airport in Atlanta. There a central terminal is linked to a series of separate concourses by underground passages with moving walkways in them. Now, the advantage of this is that any number of of extra concourses can be added away into the distance, so to speak, as . . as long as space allows. Access to the aircraft is directly through these concourses, there's no remote parking there. At Frankfurt Airport in Germany there are very long concourses joined to a big central terminal allowing access to all aircraft all along each pier. Now, the basis of this is a Y-shaped concourse with room along it for shops, bars and so on. Now, the good thing about this is that you can get to all parts of the terminal and the concourse on foot, or of course by moving walkway, and sort of s . . see the sights . . haha . . go window-shopping as you're hanging around waiting, you're not isolated in a satellite, not until you go through into your departure lounge. Now, at the moment, there's just one Y-shaped concourse with two longer piers on either side without the branches at the end – these are planned for later if they're needed. Now, a more modern airport is Charles de Gaulle in Paris, which is actually two airports. Airport One has a circular central terminal surrounded by a road with .. er .. sort of tubes carrying passengers under the road and the tarmac to several very remote-feeling satellites. Airport Two has road access inside it and is itself separated into two separate arc-shaped terminals with adjoining aircraft stands. Now, the only way to get between Airports 1 and 2 and even between A and B in Terminal 2 is by bus, or a long walk across a car park, it's very confusing for the uninitiated traveller and it is a very busy airport. Now, airports with less traffic can concentrate on convenience for the passenger, instead of 'processing' as many as possible with the least delay. Now, a good example of this is Dulles Airport in Washington. There .. ha .. remote aircraft stands are serviced by mobile departure lounges.

Presenter: Well, you're going to have to explain that to me I think!

Mark: Yes, of course, well .. er .. try and picture this: there's a central terminal with a number of adjacent departure lounges, you go through the gate, sit down in the departure lounge and when everyone is through the gate, the whole lounge drives you off to your plane on the other side of the airfield or wherever it is. It's great convenience but .. er .. it's only feasible at a not-terribly-busy airport

– imagine departure lounges moving around at Heathrow, just couldn't do it! Finally, where space is available, a number of entirely separate terminals can be built side by side, as at .. er .. King Khalid Airport in Riyadh. Now, this has three triangular terminals, each self-contained with its own facilities, and more can be added as required.

Presenter: Now, a .. a big question in the average traveller's mind is: how long does it take to get from the city to these airports?

Mark: Well .. haha .. obviously it depends on the distance from the town and also the transport facilities available. The best though is Frankfurt, which is only 10 kilometres from the town and there are plenty of fast trains. Also at Riyadh, which is only 2 kilometres from the centre, a taxi can get there very quickly. In Atlanta, if the traffic's flowing smoothly, you can cover the 11 kilometres to the airport in 20 minutes or so. Gatwick's only half an hour from London by train, even though it's 45 kilometres away. Washington's airport is also 45 kilometres away but the coach may take a long time to get there. And the worst of all: Charles de Gaulle, 25 kilometres from the city but the coach can very easily get snarled up in traffic. The nearby rail station is only reachable by bus and the journey may be crowded, and Parisian taxis are not cheap.

Presenter: So the sophisticated airport designs may be let down by surface transport that hasn't yet entered the jet age?

Mark: I'm afraid so.

(Time: 6 minutes 50 seconds)

Discussion ideas   Describe your local airport's design. Which is the worst airport you've been to? And the nicest? What do you enjoy and dislike about using an airport? And flying?

149

16.8　Margarine – a triumph of technology *Listening*

A difficult one! At least two playings needed, but note that there's no need to 'understand' all the technical terms to do the exercise.

Answers

Top row:	1	13	8	12	3rd row:	2	5	6
2nd row:	10	11	4	3	4th row:	9	7	14

Transcript

Margarine, especially the kind that's made from vegetable oils like . . er . . sunflower seeds or corn has a very good image these days. For one thing it's supposed to be better for you than animal fats, people talk about less cholesterol, that word that's very fashionable these days, and . . er . . another reason is the sunny, natural taste seems attractive to people who care about their health. But just how natural is it? Well, let me explain the process step by step. All the seeds are heated firstly and then crushed to release the oil. Now this is a . . a sort of crude plant oil and it still contains impure resins and gums. So, what you have to do next is to add caustic soda. This removes waste products in the form of soap. It may surprise you to know that a lot of the soap that's used is in fact derived by this method. The next step we have is to add fullers earth, now this bleaches it and so what you've got now is refined oil. Next, the oil has to be reacted with hydrogen plus a catalyst, in this case nickel, and this process hardens the oils. So, the following things have to

be done: they have to be neutralised, bleached yet again, and filtered to remove any waste products. Now, at this stage there is often a very nasty smell and you take this smell away by heating the hardened oils until they melt again and then when you've mixed them with fish and animal oils you've got blended oils ready to make margarine. But there are more essential ingredients to be added. You must add some water, skimmed milk, some salt and you also have to put some flavour, artificial flavour, into this tasteless mixture and make it a nice yellow colour and put in some vitamins. But you're still not quite ready, even after this lengthy process – the ingredients won't blend until they're emulsified. Now this is done by adding lecithin and monoglyceride and cooling it and mixing it all together. Now, at last, finally, it's ready to be extruded into a plastic tub and a lid with pretty sunflowers is plonked on the top. So, that's your margarine. Butter, on the other hand, is simply made by churning cream. It's pure, it's natural and it's delicious too.

(Time: 3 minutes)

Discussion ideas

How is butter 'bad for you'? Which do you eat: butter or margarine? Why? Use the rearranged pictures to explain the manufacturing process in your own words.

16.9 Ionisers
Pronunciation

Student A looks at activity 32, while B looks at 43. Both passages are extracts from the same brochure describing a particular brand of ionisers. If necessary, give help with the pronunciation of tricky words like *ions*, *impending, lethargy, prosaic, aggravated, emitting* and *conducive*.

After you have commented on students' pronunciation, get them to identify the source of the texts. Where are they taken from? What stylistic clues are there within the texts that reveal their source? Do they think that both of the extracts come from the same source?

16.10 Negative ions
Communication activity

Student A has one part of an informative cartoon strip from *The Observer* describing some of the effects of negative ions (in activity 33). Student B has the other part of the strip in 68. Both have questions to ask the other to elicit specific information.

16.11 Writing against the clock
Composition

It's important in the exam not to waste time and not to panic, of course. But it's also important to use the time you do have wisely – making notes before you start writing is one way of ensuring your composition is of a high standard, and it's not usually wasted time. Does everyone agree? The composition is best done as homework, but should be discussed in class afterwards. Was the hour too short, or too long? What would you have done differently if you could do the composition again?

Point out that one of the things you'll be looking out for is ACCURACY OF GRAMMAR AND SPELLING. 'Silly' mistakes can easily be corrected by checking your work through carefully (see 17.11). Inaccuracy may make it difficult for a reader to understand what you're trying to say, or it may distract the reader from the content of your essay. Perhaps get students to look at each other's work before it's handed in to see if there are any mistakes that can be easily spotted and put right.

N.B. If your students are doing the Listening and Interview papers some weeks before the written papers, make sure that they have a chance to do a mock listening test and a mock interview (perhaps using exercises 18.6 and 18.7) *before* they get to unit 18.

17 Nature

17.1 Vocabulary

Perhaps begin by 'brainstorming' using the board. Get everyone to write up the names of all the different animals, plants and trees they can think of in English. Which do they like or fear most? Which are endangered species? Students can work in pairs or small groups, telling one of their number to write on the board with the chalk or marker you've provided for them.

Answers   1 endangered   2 wiped out   3 breeding
4 accepted   5 fossils   6 naturalist
7 replaced (regenerated?)   8 worked up   9 wither   10 recycled
11 species   12 rodents   13 reptiles   14 deciduous trees
15 scavengers   16 prey   17 vermin   18 domesticated
19 claws   20 plumage   21 feelers   22 caterpillar   23 flock
24 mushrooms   25 endearing

Discuss why the wrong answers are incorrect in the 25 questions. Choosing the correct answer in a multiple choice question often involves eliminating the incorrect ones, just as much as selecting the correct one.

17.2 Whales   *Reading*

The questions in this exercise include some that are 'tricky' or certainly debatable. The exam itself may have some such questions, however, so it's as well to be prepared for this.

Answers   1 more animals go on dying than are born (*or* too
few new animals are born?)   2 the hunting will
stop when whales become rare   3 absurd   4 isolated   5 in the
company of many other whales   6 no guarantee that any of them would
breed   7 being adaptable   8 a distinct possibility

Discussion ideas   How can the whales, and other endangered
species, be saved? Why is it important that
they don't become extinct?

17.3 Zoos   *Reading*

Background   Gerald Durrell runs his own zoo in Jersey. He is a
well-known broadcaster and zoologist. His many
books are mostly about his encounters with animals and are full of amusing
anecdotes. Best known are *My Family and Other Animals* and *The Bafut
Beagles*. *The Stationary Ark* (1967) is one of his more serious books.

Answers   1 its being much more than a place of entertainment   2 approve of safari parks
3 frequently become ill   4 for the long-term benefit of animals
5 inadequately trained   6 at a premium   7 where wild animals are
killed off   8 improved   9 dangerously reduce their numbers in the
wild   10 zoo lover

Discuss how, by looking carefully at the questions before reading the
passage, one can often predict the answers that look most plausible. This
can save time in the exam, but BEWARE because the most plausible-
looking answer is often put there to distract you from the right one! Don't
jump to conclusions!

Discussion ideas   Where do you stand on zoos and safari parks?
Is your local zoo one of the 'excellent' ones,
or 'inferior' or 'appalling'?

17.4 Gap-filling   *Use of English*

The passage in 17.6 is the continuation of this one.

Answers   1 difficult   2 unknown   3 day
4 beneath/under   5 evening   6 screen/
sheet   7 collect/gather   8 creatures/animals/insects   9 as
10 like   11 enormous/huge/immense   12 know   13 single/pick
14 species   15 contain   16 anywhere   17 exist
18 thousands   19 careful   20 bitten/attacked

Discuss what kind of strategies one can use to 'guess' any missing words
that don't spring to mind at once. Is it best to press on and leave a gap, in the
hope that an understanding of the whole passage will help to get the words
you're not sure of? Is it better to make a wild guess than to leave a blank
space?

17.5 Idioms with RUN and STAND *Use of English*

Answers

1 I'll just run over some of the reasons why . . .
2 They can't run to setting up a nature reserve on this site.
3 Could you run off this magnificent picture of a lion for me?
4 The zoo ran into a lot of difficulty in getting the pandas to mate.
5 Time is running out if we want to save the whales.
6 As animals can't speak in their own defence, we must stand up for them. *or* As animals can't stand up for themselves, we must support them.
7 Do you know what the abbreviation RSPCA stands for?
8 It's high time the government stood out against hunting.
9 When it comes to poisoning . . . mice, it's hard to stand back from the issue.
10 It stands out a mile/stands to reason that rare species . . . need protection.

17.6 Charles Darwin *Questions and summary*

As suggested in the Student's Book, the whole of this exercise should be done in 50 minutes, which is about the time that should be devoted to it in the exam (though more time may be available if the previous Use of English exercises haven't taken too long). Is it best to do the questions and summary *first* in the exam?

Answers

1 surveying different parts of the world   2 he was astounded   3 they have not and will not change   4 he was a firm believer in God   5 they were similar to mainland animals, but different in certain details   6 came up again   7 length of necks suited available vegetation – dry islands: long necks; wet islands: short necks   8 on rafts of vegetation carried across from South America   9 deep imaginative understanding   10 it was new and changed our view of the world   11 newly-hatched baby tortoises   12 not quickly, after 25 years of work on it   13 another naturalist was about to publish a book proposing the same idea   14 given it new dimensions but not changed it in essence
15 One species can change into another; species change to suit their environment as generation succeeds generation; most efficient offspring will survive better than less efficient ones (eg tortoises with short necks in times of drought); the characteristics of the former will be transmitted to their offspring; so, perhaps, amphibians evolved from fish millions of years ago and so on.

Section A is best answered on the first listening, sections B and C on the second.

Answers

A and B   3 Brontosaurus – 20 m   8   Pterodactylus – 0.3 m
5 Diplodocus – 25 m   1   Pteranodon – 8 m
2 Ichthyosaurus – 9 m   4   Stegosaurus – 7 m
7 Procomsognathus – 1 m   9   Triceratops – 9 m
6 Plesiosaurus – 12 m   10 Tyrannosaurus – 14 m

C   1 amphibious   2 herbivorous   3 Tyrannosaurus
4 temperatures fell

Transcript

Presenter: . . . next question is from Mrs Laura Hicks of Bromley. Mrs Hicks wants to know if all dinosaurs were as huge and fierce as they're depicted in films. Bruce, perhaps you could start us off here?

Bruce: Yes, well first of all, it's . . er . . it's all conjecture really. The only evidence we've got to go on is . . er . . fossil remains and a study of bone sizes and shapes. Mrs Hicks, I'd like to say that some dinosaurs were indeed very fierce. Take the huge Tyrannosaurus: now that was 5 metres high and 14 metres long and was a carnivore. And other carniverous dinosaurs were actually much smaller. Er . . for example, the Procomsognathus was just one metre long and it actually walked on its hind legs, as did the Tyrannosaurus. But . . er . . oddly enough the really huge ones were probably not quite so fierce. The longest of all, the Diplodocus, 25 metres in length in fact, ate vegetation and it had a long tapering tail rather like a mouse's tail. And a . . the similar size and weighted dinosaur, the Brontosaurus – 20 metres in length, had a shorter, more stubby stumpy tail.

Now, both these felt as at home in water as on land. And the Brontosaurus was also a herbivore. Er . . and they were also both very timid in nature. Another herbivorous monster was the Stegosaurus, that was 7 metres in length with big triangular bony plates along the back to cool itself and also to heat itself, and this had sharp spikes on its tail – had a very small brain actually, weight of about 70 grams. Er . . talking about brains, the . . in fact the cleverest, brainiest of all was the Triceratops, who . . whose brain weighed a whole kilogram. Now, that's the one with the three horns and a bony frill round its neck. This was . . er . . 9 metres long and weighed in at 9 tons, Mrs Hicks, quite a weight. Er . . that too was indeed a herbivore and no doubt a ferocious fighter if it was attacked and . . er . . and a clever one too.

Presenter: Thank you, Bruce. Mary?

Mary: Well, not all dinosaurs were land-based. Some spent all their time in the sea. For example, the Ichthyosaurus which was 9 metres long and it had a long pointed jaw with lots of sharp teeth and it ate fish.

Then there was the Plesiosaurus, which was 12 metres long with a very long neck, and that ate fish too. Now, there were dinosaurs too in the air. The Pteranodon had a huge wingspan of 8 metres and had long pointed jaws with a bony crest on top of its head and its wings stretched between the fifth finger and body, a bit like a bat. Now, it must have been an awesome sight. But others were more like smallish birds, like Pterodactylus with a wingspan of 300 millimetres – looked like a bird in silhouette but it had sharp teeth in its beak, but it was neither fierce nor huge. Probably, therefore, most land-based dinosaurs were the smaller sort, running around between the legs of the huge ones, perhaps?

Presenter: And how about the reasons for the disappearance of the dinosaurs? Bruce?

Bruce: Well, again . . ah . . who can be sure about this? But it's often thought that some sort of global catastrophe is perhaps the reason. A meteor storm perhaps, w . . you know, a giant meteor crashing into the ocean may perhaps have raised the temperatures so much that they . . these . . these creatures couldn't survive.

Mary: Well, no. Much more likely to have been a fall in temperatures. As the climate got cooler, large reptiles would be unable to maintain body heat. The smaller ones could hide in holes during cold spells, or could take to the sea. But it's all a mystery really.

Bruce: Yeah, well, I have to . . er . . I have to concede Mary's idea is actually backed up by the survival of the modern reptiles, which we find do actually live in water or . . or in holes or . . or burrows, what you like, you know, things like crocodiles or turtles, tortoises and . . and lizards.

Presenter: Well, thank you both. Now, for our next question from Mr Ray Marsh of Chipping Sodbury . . .

(Time: 4 minutes 10 seconds)

Discussion ideas   Previous knowledge helps in doing an exercise like the one above – but in the exam topics are chosen to give no special advantages to candidates who have special knowledge. Bearing this in mind, what strategies have the members of the class developed to deal with listening comprehension tests or exercises? Get everyone to explain what they do when faced with what may turn out to be a difficult listening tape.

17.8 Worm technology   *Listening*

Play the recording twice, with a pause of 15 seconds or so before you start each playing: 'exam conditions'!

Answers   1 6m   2 (d)   3 indispensable
4 decaying plant matter   5 mix   6 four
7 land reclamation from the sea   8 low quality paper manufacture *only*
9 beef is cheaper   10 Japan

Transcript

Presenter: Earthworms are among the most common of invertebrates and among the most useful to man, as Max Wilson explains.

Max: Thank you, yes . . um . . er . . the . . the worm you usually see on . . on the grass after rain for example, er . . that is the common earthworm, Lumbricus Terrestris, and it lives on dead plant matter and grows up to 30 centimetres. Ah . . no, actually others in Australia . . er . . grow up to 3 metres and in South Africa some of them up to 6 metres. Now, like other worms it's an annelid, that means that its body is made of segments – about 150 of them, with the mouth at one end and bristles on each segment to help it to move along and it breathes through its skin and it has five hearts. I think that's about all the details of it. Now, the earthworm takes in vegetable matter and soil through its mouth and extracts vegetable matter before it excretes the remains of the soil. The worm is therefore extremely useful to man because without it gardening and agriculture would be impossible . . er . . they help keep the soil in good condition, for example by . . er . . by breaking it up into fine particles . . er . . by mixing in plant material, by bringing mineral-rich soil up to the surface and . . er . . by increasing the oxygen content of the soil. Er . . for . . for example, where demolition has taken place or land has been reclaimed . . er . . the process of making the soil suitable for growing things, er . . things to eat or plants for recreation areas, can be speeded up by adding worms to the soil and letting them get on with their business. Um . . er . . by the way, one hectare of land contains up to 5 million worms.

Presenter: Oh, I say, haha.

Max: Yes, I thought you might be interested in that. Er . . worm technology now is developing. Er . . in the first place, they can be used to turn rubbish and solid human waste into fertiliser, natural compost, and the right species can do this quicker than bacteria developing naturally according to recent experiments. Er . . secondly, they can be used to recycle waste paper to make newsprint or cardboard. A . . and thirdly they can be bred, fed on waste products, to produce animal foods . . er . . not . . not live worms: d . . dead, dried and powdered. And they're very nutritious: er . . 15% fat and they have . . er . . 45% protein, which is really a very high proportion. Um . . and fourthly they may even – this may frighten you a little bit – they . . they may even be food for humans too. Um . . at present they're more expensive than beef, but one day there may even be wormburgers . . haha . . well, you never know. It . . it sounds like a joke but in Tokyo there are in fact two restaurants which serve nothing but worm dishes. N . . absolutely true!

Presenter: Well, I hope that report from Max Wilson hasn't put you off your dinner. Time now for the weather forecast: over to Jack Welch at the weather centre . . .

(Time: 3 minutes 10 seconds)

Discussion ideas   What is the strangest thing you've ever eaten? What was it like? Do you eat a lot of meat? Do you think you ought to be a vegetarian? Could you kill an animal with your own hands if you wanted to eat it?

157

17.9   Are you an animal lover?   *Picture conversation*

Student A has a photograph of a dolphin performing (in activity 35);
student B has a sentimental painting of a lovable pony being fed by some
charming children (in activity 70). Each has questions to ask the other about
the emotions and opinions aroused by the pictures.

17.10   The jungle   *Communication activity*

Looking at activities 34 and 69, each student has some discussion-provoking
pieces of information about the progressive destruction of rain forests
(jungles) in tropical areas and about the consequences of this. Encourage
them to absorb the information and reproduce it in their own words, not to
read it aloud. This will be the best thing to do in the exam too, of course.

17.11   Practice under exam conditions   *Composition*

Remind students that in the exam they are given an impression mark for
each composition. This is based on 'an overall impression of the language
used, including the range and appropriateness of vocabulary, sentence and
paragraph structure and correctness of grammar, spelling and punctuation'.
   Give marks for the completed compositions according to these criteria:

18–20	EXCELLENT	Error-free, substantial and varied material, resourceful and controlled in language and expression.
16–17	VERY GOOD	Good realisation of task, ambitious and natural in style.
12–15	GOOD	Sufficient assurance and freedom from basic error to maintain theme.
8–11	PASS	Clear realisation of task, reasonably correct and natural.
5–7	WEAK	Near to pass level in general scope, but with numerous errors or too elementary in style.
0–4	VERY POOR	Basic errors, narrowness of vocabulary.

For more guidance on how marks are awarded, see *Cambridge Proficiency
Examination Practice 1*, Teacher's Book (CUP, 1984).
   What particular aspect of each student's composition writing needs to
be improved to be sure of doing well in the exam?

18 Living in society

These exercises can all be done under exam conditions:
18.1 and 18.2 (three passages) together in 1 hour
18.3, 18.4 and 18.5 together in 1 hour 20 minutes
18.6 (four parts) in about 40 minutes – playing each part twice with
   20 second pauses between
18.7 (three sections) in about 15 minutes
18.8 (two compositions) in 2 hours

Advice to students, exam tips and strategies are suggested below.

One tip that applies to every part of the exam is this: read the rubric in each exam paper carefully, and don't panic if you're confronted with a new type of question you haven't practised before. Expect the unexpected!

18.1 Vocabulary and usage

Advice to students: eliminating the incorrect answers may help you to discover the correct one; don't spend too long puzzling out a tricky question – mark it in pencil and come back to it later; do the easy questions first; if a question is impossible, make a guess (you've got a 1 in 4 chance of being right!) or come back to it after doing the Reading passages; choosing the 'best' answer may sometimes mean deciding which is the least bad one!

Answers

1 contribution   2 gangs   3 spectators
4 team   5 get together   6 loner
7 half-hearted   8 call upon   9 apprenticeship   10 even though
11 depends upon   12 should see   13 has broken   14 man-slaughter   15 conned   16 enforce   17 assault   18 bail
19 sentence   20 put away   21 reprimanded   22 law-abiding
23 temptation   24 eliminate   25 guess

18.2 Reading comprehension

Advice to students: look at the questions before you read each passage; some of the questions are designed to be tricky and distract you from the right answer – so don't jump to conclusions; read each passage twice: once to get the gist and then to find the answers, marking any relevant parts in pencil that you want to come back to (if you're unsure about them); in the exam each correct answer gains **two** marks; so give the tricky parts a third reading if you're still not sure of an answer.

1 they attack people in the assumed safety of their homes   2 try not to be touched   3 hostile to them   4 paradox   5 contract

6 weren't interested in hearing about his dreams   7 do not enjoy their dreams   8 people you or I might know   9 greater fear, despair and joy   10 each dream is a tangible part of our experience

11 fascinating   12 she was worried sick   13 her hostage grabbed her   14 been shot herself   15 solvent

Discussion ideas   Which of the answers given above do you disagree with? (They contain a higher proportion of debatable ones than is normal in the exam, but distinguishing between shades of meaning or choosing the best of four equally 'true' answers is a necessary exam skill – unfortunately!) What should you do if, for example, two of the alternatives seem equally OK?

18.3 Transformations   *Use of English*

Advice to students: do the easier ones first; double check each answer for grammatical accuracy and spelling; make sure you haven't unwittingly changed the meaning; return to any difficult ones later – you may have got inspiration by then!

Answers

1   Whenever we meet again/in the future, we'll always remember these days together.
2   Much as I admire her achievements, I loathe her as a person.
3   If he hadn't been reprimanded, he wouldn't be feeling so upset.
    or If he's feeling upset, it's because he was reprimanded.
4   I'd rather you admitted that you are (were?) to blame and didn't try to conceal it.
    or I'd rather you admitted that you're to blame rather than trying to conceal it.
5   Only later did I realise that I had been conned.
6   Due to the recent increase in (the number of) robberies, the police are advising vigilance.

7   There is little likelihood of his being convicted of the offence.
   or There is not much chance of his being/that he will be . . .
8   Imagine my surprise/astonishment when a policeman appeared at the
   door.
9   Unless the prosecution can produce more evidence, they have a very
   weak case.
10 I wish he hadn't sounded so half-hearted when he said he was delighted.
   or I wish he'd said he was delighted with more sincerity.

Discuss any plausible alternatives. In the exam there are often several
acceptable answers to some of the transformation questions. Expect there to
be some 'tricks' to catch you out too, as in the questions you've just done.

18.4   Fill the gaps   *Use of English*

Advice to students: as for 18.3.

Answers

1 though the test/exam was   2 for fear of
3 live up to   4 must have been   5 small
as/though   6 committing/that he had committed   7 have I heard
of/read about   8 Nevertheless/Nonetheless/However/In spite of this, *etc.*
in escaping/in getting away   9 to living   neither did/nor did   10 a
poor/an unfair/an ineffective way of testing, *etc.*

Discuss any other plausible answers. What may be difficult in this type of
test is fathoming out what is in the examiners' minds. Returning to the
tricky ones later may help you to get inspiration.

18.5   Questions and summary   *Use of English*

Section B of the Use of English paper is worth 40 to 45 per cent of the marks
for the whole paper. Aim to spend about 50 minutes on it and no longer
than an hour. Perhaps do it before section A?

Advice to students: underline all the vocabulary in pencil in the passage;
make notes before you put pen to paper – space is limited and there may be
no room for extensive corrections later; do the easier questions first and
come back to the harder ones later; if time is running out, answers in note
form are better than blank spaces; the answers have to be 'coherent and
relevant' so check for any irrelevancies in your answers, especially in the
summary; if you can rephrase some of the information in your own words
in your summary do so – if not, don't waste too much time trying to replace
every word with a synonym!

1   they had no inkling of her 'lonely decision'
2   the unemployed
3   terrified, nervous at the prospect of teaching
4   not with complete success ('patchy')
5   floating on the air
6   they became bossy, noisy and empty-headed . . .
7   a teenage magazine
8   tell him off, complain about his behaviour
9   she would have had to stay in herself too (no corporal punishment allowed)
10 the teaching staff of the school
11 they say hello and carry on messing about
12 free time when it is too rainy for the children to go out into the playground
13 the stamina and liking for being a teacher
14 ten years ago she could manage well enough; she likes children; she loves her subject; children now are different: bored, over-stimulated by too much video-watching and tired the next day, not fed properly by their parents, precociously interested in smutty side of sex, pressures of empty-headed children on hard-working ones, pressures of advertising, disruptive members of the class, bad language and behaviour, disobedient; parents unable to cope

Discussion ideas   Although the summary question at the end is only worth less than a third of the total for section B, it's probably the hardest. How can notes and any special strategies help to make the task easier? How can you make sure you haven't omitted any important points or included any irrelevant ones?

18.6   Listening comprehension

(about 40 minutes)

Play each part twice with a 20 second pause between each playing. (Don't forget to reset the counter to 000 so that you can find the beginning of each one!)

Advice to students: read all the questions before you start listening; answer all the easy questions during the first listening and save the harder ones for the second listening; don't leave any blanks – if necessary, make a guess if you really don't know an answer; beware of distractingly plausible answers, particularly ones that your common sense tells you are right but which the speakers contradict – remember it's what the speakers say that matters, not what you already know about the topic!

FIRST PART: The English pub

Answers	1 companies with various business interests

1 companies with various business interests
2 take part in a game 3 scornful
4 attract customers of all ages who have money 5 both young and old customers 6 is decorated in a style suggested by its name 7 an employee of the brewery 8 are interested in the local community
9 the fact that it's a second home 10 the noise and smoke

Transcript

18.6 Listening exercises. There are four recordings for you to listen to in this unit. Your teacher will play each part twice.
First part: The English pub.
In this recording David Rees, the writer, is being interviewed about pubs – a subject on which he is an expert.

David: When you go into a pub and buy a pint, you're not just getting a drink, you're buying your way into a sort of club and what's important in a club? The atmosphere. And it's the same with any good pub. Now, what do you get for the price of a pint? You get the smile from the landlord or the barmaid, if you're lucky, a chance to have a sandwich or play a game of darts . . a . . opportunity to find a quiet corner and . . and chat to your friends or perhaps stand at the bar and talk to the landlord or meet a stranger, make new friends. But for the brewers nowadays profit is the driving force. Did you know that 80% of the beer sold in the UK is made by only seven big companies? These . . these are conglomerates now they're not just in the business of selling beer. The highest profits are on the sale of spirits, soft drinks and lager. Now there's 50% more profit on lager than traditional bitter, you know what I mean, that lager masquerading under

Continental trade names: Heineken, Carlsberg, Skol – that have no resemblance whatsoever to any known European beer. They're weaker and have got far less flavour than the traditional English beer. But a great deal of advertising is devoted to selling these more profitable lines.

Interviewer: Before you get carried away there, David, um . . how does this affect the social role of pubs in a community?

David: Ah yes, that's very important, you see, because the . . the profitability of selling to the better-off members of society . . er . . brewers think they have to have a trendy . . a trendy young image. The worse excesses are visible in tarted-up revamped pubs . . er . . not . . not the small local ones, but I m . . the ones in prime sites: those that attract passing motorists in the country or . . or young people having a night out in the city. Ya . . for example, they even put discos in some revamped pubs. Now, the worst of all: there are these theme pubs replacing old locals with their mixed clientele of young and old, leaving the older customers nowhere to drink.

Interviewer: Wh . . what exactly do you mean by 'theme pubs'?

David: Oh well, let me tell you. The worst I've heard of: it's called the

163

Honeycomb and its interior is done out as the inside of a beehive, with even the cash register hidden under a plastic hive – can you imagine? Oh, though even worse perhaps, there's one called the Carousel. Now, the inside of this monstrosity represents a fairground with a miniature roundabout going slowly round in its centre! Well, compared with these, the Charlie Chaplin near where I live, which has mementoes of Chaplin and a black and white decor, seems almost tasteful. What else annoys me is the policy of brewers replacing their tenants – the landlord to you and me . . er . . the landlord, who in the pub is a . . is a tenant of the brewery, he pays them a rent – in replacing these with employed managers, who have no interest in the community only in securing their jobs and getting a high commission on sales. Some landlords it . . it's true are . . they're sour and unpleasant but the average manager has to do what his bosses tell him, he's not independent like a tenant landlord.

Interviewer: Yes, I see. So, wh . . what is your . . your own favourite kind of pub? The kind that shouldn't be allowed to die?

David: Well . . well, there are two sorts really, aren't there? First of all, there's the country pub. This is, you know, in a village: it's unspoilt, old of course, stone floors with . . with barrels behind the bar with taps on to serve beer by gravity not carbon dioxide. Above all and most important, it's g . . it's got local people in it, old and young people, treating the place like their homes. It . . it's cosy and warm, it may even have a log fire in the winter. Then there's the town pub, personified perhaps by a . . a London pub let's say. Now, this is completely different, it . . it's smoky, crowded . . er . . it's noisy with conversation, arguments. As you make your way through to the bar you can hear jokes on one side, anecdotes on the other. And you look around, there . . there's polished wood and brass with a row of shining bottles behind the bar. You see, a pub must be a place where both locals and strangers feel welcome and for that it must have the right atmosphere. Now, this atmosphere depends on a combination of things . . er . . of the decor, the . . the attitude of the staff and . . and their relationship with the customers. It's a centre of the community as . . as you said earlier. A village or a suburb without a pub is in my opinion a place without a heart.

Interviewer: David Rees, thank you very much. And as they're open now, perhaps you'd like to join me for a quick one . . .

(Time: 5 minutes 15 seconds)

SECOND PART: Looking for a job?

Answers

Ticks beside numbers: 1 5 6 7 10 11 12 13 14 15 18 20

Transcript

18.6 Second part: Looking for a job? In this recording advice is being given to job-seekers at the end of a seminar for university graduates.

Chairman: . . . and . . er . . we've . . er . . discussed several ideas now and . . and you've all had a chance to do some role-play of interviews, so I . . I think it's time now for our two experts to give some final tips. Er . . Kerry, let's take the application form first, because that's the first hurdle, isn't it?

Kerry: Yes, yes, that is the first hurdle. Um . . now . . er . . my suggestion may sound silly but . . er . . it's not. What you should do is . . is actually photocopy the application form and practise filling in the copy so that you don't make any mistakes . . er . . when you do the final version. Um . . this helps to . . and also type the final version . . er . . this will impress whoever's reading it and . . er . . always use the space provided, don't . . you know, don't go on, don't exceed the space that you're . . you're given, now this is important as well. Um . . you may not know this but 95% of applicants are rejected on the basis . . on the basis of the application form alone, it's very important. You see . . um . . people are so overworked, the selectors don't have time to read everything. Er . . there . . there may be 100 applicants for . . for the job that you go after. And so they . . they often skim the form, and they look for the important things . . er . . and the simple things: spelling, presentation and also vagueness, a lack of precision.

Ann: Mm, yes. I agree with Kerry but I would also stress that it is important to use words that actually show your interest in high achievement. Um . . now, I'll explain what I mean: er . . words like 'success', 'promotion' . . er 'ambition', 'responsibility'. It also helps if you've got something interesting or unusual to put on your form . . um . . this actually makes you stand out from the rest and it gives the interviewer something to talk to you about apart from anything else. Um . . for instance, an adventurous holiday, a holiday job that you've done . . um . . an unusual interest you've got, as long as it's not too weird, you know, that sort of thing.

Chairman: Mm, yes, I see, thanks. Now, about the interview itself . . er . . we've emphasised already the importance for the interviewee to ask plenty of questions, not just to sit there and be the passive partner. Kerry, what do you have to say about that?

Kerry: Yes, that's . . that's very true. Always be positive, don't . . um . . be confident, don't undersell yourself and always do lots of homework about the company that interviews you, find out about it, about . . everything you can about it: it . . its activities . . er . . its . . if it has any policies . . er . . that differ from other companies of that sort and its subsidiaries . . er . . even its competitors.

Ann: Mm, and the other thing to . . to really be prepared for are some surprises at the interview. I've known all sorts of things happen, I've known applicants being asked to solve *The Times* crossword or sort through today's in-tray putting letters in order of priority. Er . . the other thing that's quite common nowadays are group interviews with a few other applicants. Um . . y . . you might find that you're expected to spend a day with the personnel manager . . er . . having lunch with him, possibly even assisting him.

Chairman: Another surprise technique that sometimes happens is . . um . . to provoke the candidate, the interviewer insults him or . . or gets up starts shouting or something like that. And well wh . . what should one do if that situation arises?

Kerry: Well, I mean, it . . it's pretty obvious: don't lose your cool. You know, just . . er . . be . . er . . if you think about it, if . . if you just keep it in your mind that that might happen, you'll prob . . probably be all right but with most surprise techniques it's . . it's impossible to be prepared for them, you just . . um . . have to learn to expect the unexpected.

Ann: Yes, that's right, yes. And of

course, don't panic. The . . the best
way to prepare yourself is just to
practise being interviewed. A . . and as
Kerry said it's vital to present yourself
positively as somebody who's socially
sensitive, sparkling, has a sense of
humour, adaptable and intelligent – if
all those things are possible!

Kerry: But . . haha . . but if . . er . . if in
spite of all the advice we give you, you
. . you keep losing out . . um . . it's
always good to try the technique of
creative job searching.

Chairman: Creative job searching?
That's a new one on me!

Kerry: No well, it's quite simple and
you've probably done this sort of
thing already. Decide on the kind of
field that you want to work in and res
. . research it . . er . . do . . do plenty of

research and get in touch with the
companies in that field and . . er . . oh,
do . . do everything you can: talk to
people who work in . . in these companies . . um . . anything to show your
interest. If you can, get them to allow
you to spend a day there to see what
goes on and . . um . . who knows, in
the end . . .

Ann: They'll give you a job to keep you
quiet?! Haha.

Kerry: Haha. No but . . er . . if there's
an opening, you'd be surprised, you'll
be the person they think of to fill it.

Chairman: Kerry and Ann, that's a
great help, thanks a lot . . er . . I think
it's about time for coffee now, don't
you?

Ann: Mm, good idea.

Kerry: Mm.

(Time: 5 minutes)

THIRD PART: Rules and values

Answers 1 rules are not recorded   2 regulate people's
behaviour   3 judge   4 want to be the same
as everyone else   5 no one would know how to behave   6 share the
same values   7 they cannot be successful   8 society's rules and
values may change

Transcript

18.6   Third part: Rules and values
In this recording Dr James White, a
sociologist, is talking about how society
works.

Interviewer: Dr White, as a sociologist,
you're an expert on the patterns of
behaviour that exist in different
societies and on the rules that are
followed. What is meant by a 'rule' in
this case?

Dr White: Now, that's an interesting
question. Well, we must make a dis-
tinction between a rule and a law.
Both may have equal power but a law
is a written-down version of a rule of
behaviour. Now, to understand the
power of rules, I'll give you an exam-

ple, let's take chess. To understand
what's going on in a game of chess
you have to know the rules that are
being followed and to play you have
to follow the same rules. You have a
choice of moves to make but they
must all obey the appropriate rules,
and so likewise in society. The trouble
is that these rules may be mostly
internalised, we don't realise that
we're following them. For example,
the rules of our mother tongue, the
way we speak. Now, we don't have to
obey the rules – if we're losing a game
we can spoil it by cheating or by
refusing to continue playing.

Interviewer: Yes, but to take up your chess

analogy, we know that our aim is to win so that's the purpose of the game.

Dr White: Haha. Well don't ask me what the purpose of life is, but playing chess is also a way of organising time and interaction . . er . . the rules of society have the same purpose. If we act in ways that other people approve of, then they reward or praise us; and if we act in ways they disapprove of then they can show their disapproval or punish us by taking away our life or our freedom or our physical comfort or our goods. In Western society these punishments are all controlled by written-down laws and people who are punished are called 'criminals'. But parents or teachers may in some cases have their own rules that entitle them to punish the children that they're responsible for.

Interviewer: But surely the majority of adults conform to the rules and laws because they want to, not because they fear punishment if they don't?

Dr White: Absolutely, the strongest motive is the desire to conform. Also we're very sensitive to approval, for example we suffer an agony of embarrassment if we do something supposedly wrong in public. It's the existence of a shared set of rules that makes it possible for there to be stable patterns of social interaction. We play roles which have . . er . . different role expectations. For example, a teacher gives lessons and instructions and a pupil attends and follows. If everyone accepts the rules then any deviance is inhibited by this.

Interviewer: Another factor is the sharing of values within a society, isn't it?

Dr White: Yes, absolutely, for a complex society to operate, its members all have to subscribe to the same set of values. Values represent a consensus of what is good or right. Now, they may be part of a . . say a religious or a political system: Protestantism, social-

(Time: 4 minutes 30 seconds)

ism, capitalism, etc. For example . . um . . in the USA success is sometimes said to be the controlling value of all social endeavour . . er . . whether in work, in sport and school, whatever. Acceptance of the same values creates solidarity and unity among all the people. We associate with people who share the same values as us, well, we like them more than those who have different values.

Interviewer: Of course. No society's perfect and there are likely to be many contradictory and ambiguous rules.

Dr White: Oh sure, and no society could ever eliminate these but the fact that there is social harmony to a great extent suggests that there are many more rules and values that are shared in common. But in any society there's likely to be deviance from the rules and values. There are two ways that this deviance can manifest itself: er . . there's dropping out for example in . . in the US, where . . er . . financial success may be hard to attain by someone who is . . is poor or illiterate or has no skills. Then . . er . . dishonesty or taking drugs or getting drunk, becoming a tramp or a hobo – all these things may be ways of dropping out. Alternatively, a reaction may be to rebel, to rebel against society . . er . . substituting new values and rules. This can be considered as . . as positive, it leads to finding ways of altering values for the benefit of a changing society, or it can. But more often it's considered anti-social, for instance it manifests itself in . . er . . in street gangs and . . er . . the criminal subculture, etc.

Interviewer: Mm, though the terms positive and anti-social would be the ones used by the members of the society in question?

Dr White: Oh yes, that's right. Well, they're not objective terms.

Interviewer: Dr White, thank you.

167

FOURTH PART: Attitudes

Answers

1 angry 2 disappointed 3 impressed
4 sarcastic 5 diffident

Transcript

18.6 Fourth part: Attitudes
Listen carefully to each of the speakers
and decide what attitude each is con-
veying to the listener. Mark your
answers in your book.

ONE 'Could I have a word with you?
Yes. Well, you see, I've been looking
at your work and comparing it with . .
with what the others have been doing
and . . well, you know what I think
about everyone else's work, don't

you? I mean, it's improved a lot.
Anyway, looking at yours in compari-
son, I must say that you've really . . . I
. . I mean, yours is far and away the
most . . .'

[The same text is acted out four more
times.]

That's the end of the listening exercises
and we'd like to wish you good luck in
your exam!
Yes, good luck! Good luck!

(Time: 3 minutes 15 seconds)

Discussion ideas What seems to be the hardest thing in doing a
listening comprehension test? Staying awake
during the second listening? In the exam the test will probably only last
about half an hour, but don't expect the texts to be particularly interesting
or exciting!

18.7 Interview

If at all possible, arrange the participation of another teacher to play the role
of 'examiner', so that mock interviews can be carried out. 'Candidates'
could be interviewed in front of the rest of the class and helpful advice
offered afterwards in a follow-up discussion.

Remind everyone that candidates are assessed in the exam on their:
FLUENCY and GRAMMATICAL ACCURACY,
PRONUNCIATION OF INDIVIDUAL SOUNDS and SENTENCES (stress and
intonation),
INTERACTIVE COMMUNICATIVE ABILITY and VOCABULARY RESOURCE.

Advice to students: don't be the passive partner – take the initiative just as
you would in a normal conversation; let the examiner hear a reasonable
sample of your spoken English; remember that it's how you communicate
that's being assessed, not whether your answers are correct, intelligent or
sensible – or even true!

Photograph
Students can 'interview' each other. Student A has a picture of a street scene in activity 36; student B has a picture of an elderly couple asleep in deckchairs in activity 72. Each has questions to ask the other.

Reading passage
Each student has half of a short newspaper article about the abolition of homework in Spanish schools to comment on, refer to and discuss. Student A has the first half in activity 24, student B the second half in activity 41.

Communication activity
Students can work in groups of three or pairs, or with an 'examiner' as partner. The starting point is the information on page 253.

Discussion afterwards

Advise each student what strengths he or she should be aware of and what weaknesses he or she might be able to work on before the exam itself. The best advice is probably to 'be yourself' and try not to be too nervous.

18.8 Composition

Advice to students: read all the questions through carefully (TWICE!); make sure you answer the questions as they are asked, not as you'd like them to be; check all your work through thoroughly to eliminate all the silly mistakes you may have made; write clearly and leave plenty of room for yourself to make corrections later (extra paper is free!); make notes before you start writing; be prepared for a 'surprise item' – like the 150-word limit in no. 3!
Use the marking scheme suggested in 17.11 when you mark the completed compositions.

Envoi

Before the members of the class do the exam, allow time for them to try doing a couple of practice exams from *Cambridge Proficiency Examination Practice 1*. They will also certainly appreciate some pre-exam tips – repeat the advice suggested at the beginning of each exercise here in unit 18. Above all, urge them to stay calm, use their time wisely and do their best! Oh, and give them my best wishes too!

Leo Jones